The Beginning of Baptist Ecclesiology

Monographs in Baptist History

VOLUME 6

Ours is a day in which not only the gaze of western culture but also increasingly that of Evangelicals is riveted to the present. The past seems to be nowhere in view and hence it is disparagingly dismissed as being of little value for our rapidly changing world. Such historical amnesia is fatal for any culture, but particularly so for Christian communities whose identity is profoundly bound up with their history. The goal of this new series of monographs, Studies in Baptist History, seeks to provide one of these Christian communities, that of evangelical Baptists, with reasons and resources for remembering the past. The editors are deeply convinced that Baptist history contains rich resources of theological reflection, praxis and spirituality that can help Baptists, as well as other Christians, live more Christianly in the present. The monographs in this series will therefore aim at illuminating various aspects of the Baptist tradition and in the process provide Baptists with a usable past.

The Beginning of Baptist Ecclesiology

The Foundational Contributions of Thomas Helwys

Marvin Jones

FOREWORD BY
Malcolm B. Yarnell III

⌐PICKWICK *Publications* · Eugene, Oregon

THE BEGINNING OF BAPTIST ECCLESIOLOGY
The Foundational Contributions of Thomas Helwys

Monographs in Baptist History 6

Pickwick Publications
An Imprint of Wipf and Stock Publishers
199 W. 8th Ave., Suite 3
Eugene, OR 97401

www.wipfandstock.com

PAPERBACK ISBN: 978-1-5326-1458-3
HARDCOVER ISBN: 978-1-5326-1460-6
EBOOK ISBN: 978-1-5326-1459-0

Cataloguing-in-Publication data:

Names: Jones, Marvin. | Yarnell, Malcolm B., III, foreword.

Title: The Beginning of Baptist Ecclesiology : The Foundational Contributions of Thomas Helwys / Marvin Jones.

Description: Eugene, OR: Pickwick Publications, 2017 | Series: Monographs in Baptist History 6 | Includes bibliographical references and index.

Identifiers: ISBN 978-1-5326-1458-3 (paperback) | ISBN 978-1-5326-1460-6 (hardcover) | ISBN 978-1-5326-1459-0 (ebook)

Subjects: LCSH: Helwys, Thomas, 1550?–1616?. | Church. | Baptist—Doctrines.

Classification: BX6495.H44 J7 2017 (print) | BX6495.H44 (ebook)

Manufactured in the U.S.A.   06/14/17

This work is dedicated to those godly men who taught me the meaning and ministry of the local Baptist Church:

Dr. Paige Patterson, who taught me the foundational basics of theology and ministry. He also taught me that theology and ministry are not only compatible but necessary for the local church pastor. His contribution to me is counted as a true gift from a great man.

Dr. Alfred Wright, who demonstrated godly discipleship to me, as a young pastor, when I desperately needed a mentor. He instilled within me a desire, even passion, to preach to God's people. His admonition is still the well from which I draw deep spiritual water today. The time has come and gone and the miles between us are many but he always has a place in my heart and is often on my mind.

Dr. Malcolm Yarnell, patiently and persistently mentored me at the academic level. He spent countless hours with me in conversation, luncheons, emails, and phone conversations. He encouraged me to "dig deep" and "exercise my theological muscle." His friendship is a blessing not only to me but to all who know him.

Rev. Danny Henson is a true friend and surrogate pastor to me and my family. He has given godly advice in tough situations. He demonstrated godly love in such capacity that Jesus Christ was glorified by the endeavor. He is a consummate pastor, gifted preacher, and I am blessed to call him my friend.

Contents

Contents

Baptist Ecclesiology as a Consistent Model of the New Covenant
Implications for Baptist Ecclesiology

Foreword

MARVIN JONES'S GROUNDBREAKING WORK, *The Beginning of Baptist Ecclesiology*, is important for three major reasons. First, it provides an historical and biographical introduction to the theological genius behind the early English Baptist movement. While scholarly attention has primarily centered upon John Smyth, it is significant that Thomas Helwys parted with Smyth for theological reasons that still define Baptists vis-à-vis Smyth's beloved Anabap'ism. It was not Smyth's advocacy but Helwys's rejection—his refutation *inter alia* of the need for baptismal successionism, of the exclusion of Christian magistrates from the church, and of the celestial flesh doctrine of early Dutch Anabaptism—that carried the day among later Baptists. In these significant and farsighted ways, Helwys limited and redirected Smyth's otherwise seminal impact.

Moreover, it was not Smyth but Helwys who took the nascent Baptist church back to England. Driven by Helwys's desire to reach the English-speaking peoples with the gospel—the gospel understood in a Baptist vein—the earliest London free churches precariously held onto life under intense persecution. This small, endangered community subsequently rallied forth to become a worldwide communion that includes today over 40 million people. And it is Helwys's theology of the church that has largely defined these Baptists since his time. Although Helwys's position on the extent of the atonement has not been universal among the Baptists, his ecclesiology has persuaded most Baptists and many other free churches beyond the Baptists. It is Thomas Helwys who first and lastingly articulated the Baptist vision.

The second reason that Jones's presentation of Helwys is important is that it gives us an in-depth treatment of an author and a book that has long been seen as important in Baptist history, but Jones does this in a new and compelling way. Some scholars trace the very beginning of the English Baptist movement to Helwys and consider his groundbreaking text, *A Short Declaration of the Mistery of Iniquity* (1612), as particularly important in discerning certain visions of Baptist life. Still other scholars would limit the first English Baptist pastor's influence to a minor stream of Baptist life. But Helwys's determined public witness—a witness that cost him his freedom and most likely his life—two decades prior to the emergence of other Baptist movements will continually handicap any delimiting claims. A third group of scholars are not primarily concerned with Helwys as a Baptist theologian *per se*, but as a defender of universal religious liberty. All three presentations would doubtless cause Helwys himself, a most severe prophet for godly church life, to wonder at what has been wrought with his legacy. Jones helps peel back the historiographical layers to reintroduce us to a more fundamental and complex theological character than previously envisaged.

The third and final reason that Marvin Jones's book is important is that it makes a claim that should upend the general scholarship about the particular theological importance of Helwys, especially when viewed from the perspective of Helwys's own self-understanding. Jones reads Helwys in an unusual manner but in the supremely sensible way that occurs when the available evidence is allowed to establish its own placement. He treats Helwys's most important work not primarily as an eschatological text, although that is manifestly its genre. Nor does Jones perceive *Mistery of Iniquity* to be a text primarily about religious liberty, although that is an important implication of the book. Rather, Jones receives this prophetic book as a treatise regarding the identity of the beloved church of Jesus Christ.

Jones provides a historically-aware and theologically-sensitive contextual interpretation of Helwys that should ultimately impact the scholarly view not merely of the latter's philosophy of the church-state relationship but of much else ecclesiological besides. Rather than "steal the thunder" from the author's thoughtful scholarship, I leave you with this admonition: Listen to Marvin Jones lecture on Thomas Helwys and learn to think about the epoch-making vision of the Baptists in a novel yet ancient way.

Malcolm B. Yarnell III

Research Professor of Systematic Theology
Southwestern Baptist Theological Seminary
Fort Worth, Texas

Preface

MY PERSONAL DESIRE TO reacquaint myself with Baptist ecclesiology and Baptist origins grew out of necessity. In 2008 I was asked to teach a course on Baptist history at Emanuel University in Oradea, Romania. I delved into the English Separatist and Anabaptist movements. I re-read *The Anabaptist Story* (Eerdmans, 1996) with a more critical focus. I immersed myself in Leon McBeth's *The Baptist Heritage: Four Hundred Years of Baptist Witness* (Broadman, 1987). These studies led to a proposal to Dr. Malcolm Yarnell and Dr. Paige Patterson. I shared my interest of studying with Dr. Yarnell at Southwestern Baptist Theological Seminary in order to critically examine historical Baptist ecclesiology at the doctoral research level. It was Dr. Yarnell that suggested that I review, once again, Thomas Helwys's work, *The Mystery of Iniquity.*

In order to understand the historical context of Thomas Helwys, I began to review John Smyth's life. His life, intermingling with Thomas Helwys, instilled in me a new appreciation for Helwys's ministry. Their friendship and their subsequent parting of the ways revolved around a theological and ecclesiological dynamic. They were seeking to establish or re-establish a biblical church. I slowly began to realize that Helwys was more influential upon Baptist life than previously known. Dr. Yarnell suggested that I read Helwys with a more "critical eye" than I had earlier. He and I talked about Helwys's purpose for writing *The Mystery of Iniquity.* The truth of the matter was inescapable. Helwys truly believed he had helped recover a biblical ecclesiology—the true church. Helwys compared the new-found Baptist movement to the unhealthy churches of the English Reformation, the English Separatists, the continental European Reform movement, and the Roman Catholic Church.

Knowing that most scholars regard Helwys's work, *The Mystery of Iniquity*, as a treatise dedicated to religious liberty, I knew that my conclusions about Helwys's affirmation of his own appreciation for Baptist ecclesiology would be suspect. Yet at the same time men like James Leo Garrett, Malcolm Yarnell, Michael Haykin, Nathan Finn, Jason Duesing, Peter Beck, Mark Dever, and others were giving a healthy renewed interest in Baptist ecclesiology. The renewed interest in Baptist studies allowed for a current examination of Thomas Helwys's contributions to ecclesiology.

This modern emphasis on Baptist studies gives rise to the issue of Baptist ecclesiological origins. The basic question of "where did Baptist come from and why" has two camps that offer differing explanations: 1) The Separatist camp is represented by noted historian Barrie White. His work, *The English Separatist Tradition: From the Marian Martyrs to the Pilgrim Fathers* (Oxford University Press, 1971) is an exhaustive study depicting the English Separatist movement and the logical flow and transitional thought that produced the ministry of John Smyth and Thomas Helwys. 2) The Anabaptist movement is the second camp and it is represented by capable historians like William R. Estep. His work, *The Anabaptist Story* (Eerdmans, 1996) is now in its third edition and has become the standard textbook for introductory courses on Anabaptist history. Those who espouse the Anabaptist position as the originator of the modern Baptist movement understand either a direct connection via lineage back to the infamous Swiss Brethren or an indirect connection via the Anabaptist teachings. In other words, Anabaptist ecclesiology is very much akin, if not in some ways identical, to modern Baptist ecclesiology.

My conclusions about Helwys's Baptist church are that it resembles both the English Separatist and the Anabaptist ecclesiology with notable differences with both entities. When *The Mystery of Iniquity* is properly understood, as Helwys intended, the reader will grasp the logical reasons that the Baptist church, in 1607, was akin to both the English Separatist and the Anabaptist and yet different from both English Separatism and Anabaptism. My goal in writing *The Beginning of Baptist Ecclesiology* is twofold then: 1) to give a fresh voice to Thomas Helwys's opinion that a Baptist church is a viable New Testament church, 2) to provide further relevant material in the conversation concerning Baptist origins and the rationale for their origins.

This work would not have been possible without the help, suggestions, and critique of many people. My wife Stacy and our two children, Marshall and McKenzie, and my daughter-in-law, Brittany, have been encouraging during the entire process. They are the Lord's blessing to me. One of the Lord's surprises was the inclusion of Jerry Sutton who served on my doctoral committee. After reading the manuscript for the dissertation it was he who first mentioned publishing this work. The task of taking a dissertation and making it publication-ready was a challenge but Jerry was a constant source of encouragement to me during the process. Another surprise was fellow doctoral student Matt Ward. He reviewed and edited the manuscript for publication. His skills, as is his friendship, are remarkable. I would be remiss if I do not say "thank you" to Michael Haykin for publishing the work in the series Monographs in Baptist History. He has been a constant source of blessing to me. I owe a debt of gratitude to Malcolm Yarnell for his tireless efforts of being a helpful critic, constant friend, and basic source of inspiration during my doctoral study years at Southwestern Baptist Theological Seminary. Regardless of the work and contribution of these wonderful people I admit that any errors are mine.

Marvin Jones

Louisiana College
Pineville, Louisiana

1

A Historical Review of the
Life of Thomas Helwys

Introduction

THOMAS HELWYS IS FOREVER linked to the person of John Smyth when popular consideration is given to the two men. However, the first Baptist pastor of the first Baptist church on English soil was Thomas Helwys. His pastorate was set in the foreground of the English Reformation, but he had the distinction of being ecclesiologically different from Anglicanism, Anabaptism, and the Reformed church. Helwys pastored a church that established a tradition known as Baptist. However, this Baptist identity, which developed further Baptist distinctives, demands an examination of its ecclesiological and soteriological positions. Helwys and his church differed from all ecclesiological options available at that time. He believed that his church had rediscovered the biblical truth concerning the nature of the church.

While Thomas Helwys's *A Short Declaration of the Mystery of Iniquity* has been correctly recognized as an important seminal document of the English Baptist movement and for religious liberty, it has not been recognized as an important seminal contribution to Baptist ecclesiology. Helwys's *A Short Declaration of the Mystery of Iniquity* describes improper ecclesiologies and demonstrates Baptist ecclesiology as the only true church.

The History of Religious Liberty in England
Gives Rise to the *Mystery of Iniquity*

The desire for religious toleration was abundant in seventeenth-century England. With the advent of the rule of King James I, the Puritans of the Church of England took the occasion to request toleration and mild reform from the new king as presented in the Millenary Petition. The petition was alleged to have had over a thousand signatures of Puritan clergy wanting to reform the Church of England from its Catholic ceremonies. The document also contained the assurance of the Puritan's loyalty to the king. The response of the king was the infamous Hampton Court Conference, assembled in January 1604.[1]

This conference was attended by Dr. Reynolds, one of only four Puritan ministers invited, whereas not one Separatist was extended an invitation.[2] Dr. Reynolds had sworn devotion to the king and Royal Supremacy.[3] The rationale for his allegiance was to demonstrate that the Puritans were loyal subjects of the king. Steven Wright acknowledges the following:

> During the reign of Elizabeth, official Protestantism became increasingly bound up with national identity, defined principally against that of Catholic Spain. The Anglican church was supported by the state in the defense of its monopoly of legitimate religious practice and belief, despite the variations to be found within it.[4]

King James, however, was not willing to acquiesce to Puritan reform, even though Reynolds was loyal to the crown. The conference ended with an official set of Canons enacted. The third canon affirmed the Church of England, as established under the king's jurisdiction, as a true Apostolic Church. If the Canons were denied by anyone, that person would be excommunicated. Griswold comments, "Within one year about 300 Puritan preachers were silenced and turned out of their pulpits for rejecting the ceremonies, as being popish."[5] The conference made the clear decision that the Church of England would remain without Puritan reform. Barrington White comments, "One consequence was that a number of the more radical

---

1. Jordan, *Development of Religious Toleration*, 2:18.

2. Griswold, "Congregational Dynamics," 233.

3. Cross and Livingston, *Oxford Dictionary of the Christian Church*, s.v. "Royal Supremacy."

4. Wright, *Early English Baptists*, 3.

5. Griswold, "Congregational Dynamics," 234.

wing of reforming clergy and laymen withdrew during the next years into Separatism."[6]

Separatism

The fact must be noted that the results of the Hampton Court Conference did not create Separatism.[7] The results simply made the more radically inclined Puritans willing to embrace the movement. The primary difference between Puritanism and Separatism was their respective attitudes toward the Church of England. The former accepted the position that the Church of England could be purified or reformed, whereas the latter embraced the position that the Church of England was nothing less than an English version of the corrupt Roman Catholic Church, for example, a false church. White comments:

> At the same time the similarity in ecclesiological convictions between Separatists and the more extreme Puritans made it comparatively easy for individuals to move from one position to the other. It could be reasonably held that Separatism was the logical policy for Puritans to adopt if their ideals were too long thwarted or, to put it very slightly different, when their patience was exhausted.[8]

The increase of Separatists under the new Canons resulted in the ranks of Separatism swelling numerically, along with the increasing displeasure toward the Church of England and King James.

Smyth, Helwys, and Separatism

The ministry of John Smyth must be considered in order to understand the appropriate background for Thomas Helwys's work, *A Short Declaration of the Mystery of Iniquity*. The friendship between John Smyth and Thomas Helwys was born out of the kindness of Helwys. According to Joe Early Jr., Helwys was instrumental in helping Smyth regain his health, stating, "Helwys took him to Broxtowe Hall and over several months slowly nursed him back to health."[9] It must be noted that the above incident took place in

---

6. White, *English Puritan Tradition*, 19–20.

7. For a summary of the Separatist movement, see Burrage, *Early English Dissenters*.

8. White, *English Separatist Tradition*, 33.

9. Helwys, *Life and Writings of Thomas Helwys*, 17.

1606, whereas the first meeting between the two men was in 1600.[10] Thus, their friendship developed over a six-year period.

Eventually the Puritan ideas of Smyth gave way to Separatist ideology. Helwys supported this move as he also embraced Separatism. During the year 1606 the church at Gainsborough, near Broxtowe Hall, called John Smyth as pastor. This congregational church divided into two groups to accommodate their size, which was too visible.

> The large membership of this congregation meant it could be an easy target for persecution. The first group met at Scrooby Manor House and was led by John Robinson, William Bradford, and William Brewster. The congregation became known as the Pilgrim Church. The second group was led by John Smyth and Thomas Helwys, retaining the original name of "The Gainsborough Church."[11]

The Gainsborough Church faced the possibility of persecution. Lawrence Holiday Harris states:

> Some of these Separatists were frightened by the memory of the Dissenters Barrowe, Greenwood, and Perry, who were executed in England in 1593. Led by the Gainsborough congregation in 1607, both groups migrated to Protestant Holland, a tolerant state that welcomed Separatists from about 1595 . . . the other group, from Scrooby Manor Church, led by John Robinson and layman Richard Clyfton, moved to Leyden . . .[12]

The church, now at Amsterdam, was living without the fear of persecution. Leon McBeth states that "they had formed their church on the basis of the Old Testament covenant," but they had not given much thought to the visible sign of the church or who constituted membership of the church.[13] Separatists did not embrace believers' baptism, but they did reject the origin of the Church of England. Therefore, the church at Amsterdam still adhered to the Separatist ecclesiological position. However, the church would not remain in this position for long.

---

10. Ibid., 16.
11. Torbet, *History of the Baptists*, 34.
12. Harris, *Origins and Growth of the Baptist Faith*, 4.
13. McBeth, *Baptist Heritage*, 35.

Baptists and Baptism

Smyth, who had rejected the Church of England as being a viable New Testament church, also began to question the baptism of the Church of England. The logic was if the Church of England was not a viable church, then its ordinances could not be valid. This concept was further developed as Smyth continued reading the New Testament. A. C. Underwood states:

> Examination of the New Testament convinced him that baptism upon profession of repentance towards God and faith in Christ was the New Testament method of admitting to church fellowship, and that the New Testament knew nothing of the baptism of infants. Smyth then drew the logical inference that the baptism which he and his congregation had received in the parish churches of England was worthless.[14]

The logical progression was to move toward the Baptist position. Smyth renounced his baptism by the Church of England and reconstituted the church through believers' baptism.

The question arose of how does one embrace believers' baptism if no church possesses it? The solution, for Smyth, was to baptize himself. Functionally, in order to baptize the congregation he first had to baptize himself. Jason K. Lee comments that "Smyth shocked his fellow Separatists by rejecting infant baptism and reestablishing his church through believers' baptism. The fact that, according to early accounts, Smyth had baptized himself added to their bewilderment."[15] By an act of baptizing himself and his congregation, Smyth had declared that the church was to be a believers' church, composed of those who were saved and then baptized in obedience to the Lord's command. Thomas Helwys accepted this act of baptism as he believed they had recovered a properly constituted church. The result of this action was that it produced a Baptist church. James Leo Garrett comments:

> One would hardly dispute the claim, however, that ecclesiology was Smyth's most developed doctrine. He rigorously rejected the baptism of infants, asserted that baptism should only be administered to voluntary or professed believers who are regenerate, retained the baptismal mode of aspersion or affusion, and denied that succession in the administration of baptism was necessary.[16]

14. Underwood, *History of English Baptists*, 37.
15. Lee, *Theology of John Smyth*, 71.
16. Garrett, *Baptist Theology*, 26.

Smyth embraced the principles of baptism and Baptist ecclesiology. However, this action did not settle the question of ecclesiology for Smyth. He was not satisfied that his church had been properly reconstituted, and he began to question whether his actions were biblically legitimate.

Smyth came under the conviction that it was wrong to baptize himself, especially since he was seeking a New Testament church. His goal was to find a church that had a lineage or succession back to the apostolic church. James Coggins states:

> John Smyth and many members of his congregation decided that instead of baptizing themselves they should have asked the Mennonites to baptize them . . . what they had convinced the Smyth congregation of was that the Mennonites were a true church. According to *The Character of the Beast*, a true church was one constituted by believers' baptism, and for this the Mennonites certainly qualified.[17]

To be clear, he never doubted believers' baptism but he did doubt the church's succession as a viable, apostolic New Testament church. He did not think that he could simply create a church by covenant and then administer the ordinances. Clayton states:

> Doubting the validity of his act and feeling the Mennonite Church was a true church administering true ordinances, Smyth decided that he should seek baptism from the Mennonites. Consequently, Smyth and thirty-two members of his party petitioned the Mennonites for membership in their church in February, 1609/10.[18]

At this point in time, Smyth was willing to accept that the Mennonites had a true constituted church. It was this decision that led Helwys to separate from Smyth and the rest of the congregation. He and a small group of approximately ten members withdrew from the church and excommunicated Smyth and his followers. Ernest Payne writes:

> To his [Helwys] distress he found himself at all three points [Successionism, Hoffmannite Christology, Christians and the Magistracy], disagreeing with the one whom till then he had so gladly and gratefully followed. Hoffmannite Christology was unorthodox and unsatisfactory. If the baptism [with]which they had reconstituted their fellowship was invalid, what guarantee was there that

17. Coggins, *John Smyth's Congregation*, 78.
18. Clayton, "Thomas Helwys," 6.

Mennonite baptism was correct? The whole idea of a necessary human succession was to be rejected.[19]

In order to continue as a church, Helwys believed it was necessary to defend the ecclesiology he had embraced. He immediately began to write *A Declaration of Faith of the English People Remaining at Amsterdam in Holland*. McBeth considers this work as confirmation that, "the Helwys group continued to adhere to the Baptist principles earlier announced and then abandoned by Smyth."[20]

For two years, Helwys pastored the congregation in Amsterdam, but he did not consider this a permanent solution. Helwys took the church back to Spitalfields, England, and he planted the very first English Baptist Church on English soil, thus starting the General Baptist movement within England. Wilbur Kitchener Jordan states, "The evangelical tendencies inherent in the Baptist philosophy and the persistence of feud with Smyth's followers, however, caused them in 1611 to determine to return to England."[21]

In preparing the trip back to England he wrote *A Short Declaration of the Mystery of Iniquity*. This work has been recognized as an advanced development in the call for liberty of conscience, not simply religious toleration. Jordan comments on the impact of Helwys's *Mystery of Iniquity*:

> Helwys broke new and important ground when he argued that Christian thinkers have been completely illogical about the question of religious power of the magistrate. . . . The great Baptist thinker proposed that religious liberty was the best solution for the strife and contention which had for so long beset England. He scorned legal toleration as unworthy and as derived from an authority which the State did not in fact possess. Every sect should be vested with liberty, not only of opinion but of worship.[22]

What has not been adequately recognized is that in this same work Helwys developed and defended the uniqueness of Baptist ecclesiology.

19. Payne, *Thomas Helwys*, 7.

20. McBeth, *Baptist Heritage*, 38.

21. Jordan, *Development of Religious Toleration in England*, 2:264.

22. Ibid., 276–84.

The Interpretation of *Mystery of Iniquity* in Secondary Literature

A Short Declaration of the Mystery of Iniquity has been interpreted in secondary literature as a work that calls for religious liberty. The book is entitled after Paul's phrase in 2 Thess 2:7 (KJV), which states that "the mystery of iniquity doth already work."[23] Helwys picked up on the theme of iniquity at work and applied it to the lack of religious toleration within England. Joe Early Jr. claims that the book was written in Holland and published there in late 1611 prior to the return to English soil.[24] If Early is correct then it is safe to assume that the book was also written for the church to prepare for persecution from their fellow Englishmen. Regardless of the actual recipients, the book was born out of a sense of obligation to return to England and initiate change. Clayton confirms this as he states that Helwys "became progressively convinced that he had acted improperly in fleeing England to avoid persecution."[25] A general survey of Baptist theologians and historians from the nineteenth and twentieth centuries will confirm that *A Short Declaration of the Mystery of Iniquity* has been considered to be the first English Baptist document to declare religious freedom and toleration.

Nineteenth Century

In the nineteenth century, Adam Taylor produced one of the earliest works on General Baptist history. His work, The History of the English General Baptists, was published in 1818 in London.[26] Taylor gives the account of the origin of the English Baptists and proceeds to record their ministry under the leadership of Thomas Helwys. His comments on the return of the General Baptists to England affirm the position that Helwys published his book with religious toleration in mind. Taylor states:

> But the principal glory of this piece is the manly and explicit avowal which the authors make of the true principles of Christian liberty, at a time when they were either unknown or opposed, by almost every other party. They preserve distinction between civil and religious concerns; and while they fully allow the magistrate

---

23. 2 Thess 2:7.

24. Helwys, *Life and Writings of Thomas Helwys*, 36.

25. Clayton, "Thomas Helwys," 7.

26. Taylor, *History of the English General Baptists*.

his proper authority in the former, they boldly maintain every man's right to judge and act for himself in the latter.[27]

Taylor understood the book to be a call for religious liberty based upon the premise that it was a Christian mandate. He also stated that Helwys summoned the call for religious liberty when most were opposed to such a claim.

Later in the nineteenth century, another work of importance was William Cathcart's *The Baptist Encyclopedia*. This work was an intensive focus on the Baptist movement of England. The work was published in 1881 approximately 250 years after the life of Helwys. Cathcart's entry for Thomas Helwys stated that Helwys's contribution to religious freedom was only held by Baptists.

> His views of civil government in relation to religion were thoroughly Scriptural, and in that day were held by none but Baptists. . . . Nothing more emphatic was overwritten on the question of soul liberty in any age or country. But in the days of Helwys this doctrine was denounced by Robinson, the father of the Puritans who founded New Plymouth in 1620. Mr. Helwys and his Baptist brethren were detested as much for the liberty of conscience for which they pleaded as for the believers' baptism which they practiced.[28]

The significance of this work is that an encyclopedia depicts Thomas Helwys's book as a summons for religious freedom. From an academic standpoint, this official work declares Thomas Helwys as the first of the English Baptists to understand the issue of religious freedom.

Early Twentieth Century

In the twentieth century, during the tri-centennial celebration of the first Baptist church in England, Walter Burgess, Champlin Burrage, and William T. Whitley contributed works that brought the General Baptist movement to the forefront of Baptist studies. In his doctoral dissertation, Jeong In Choi recognizes the impact of these three men's contributions.

> Walter Burgess, Champlin Burrage, and William T. Whitley provided pivotal works about the historical and theological

27. Ibid., section 3, chap. 1.
28. Cathcart, *Baptist Encyclopedia*, s.v. "Helwys, Thomas."

significance of Smyth and Helwys. Burgess, an American Unitarian historian, presented a balanced history of Smyth and Helwys in 1911. The significance of Burgess's work was his consideration of the documents of congregational forefathers such as John Robinson and William Bradford.[29]

Walter Burgess's work included the accounts of John Smyth, but continues the story with Thomas Helwys.[30]

Concerning Helwys's work, *A Short Declaration of the Mystery of Iniquity*, Burgess states:

> It is in his pleading with the King for religious liberty that we come upon some of the most dignified and eloquent passages in all the writings of Helwys. He is here lifted up by the very greatness of his theme. Almost the first, if not the first, among English writers to distinguish between temporal and spiritual authority and to define their limits, he wrote with passion on behalf of liberty for all peaceable subjects in matters of religion.[31]

Burgess does not investigate the ecclesiology of Thomas Helwys, but he continues the pattern of assigning Helwys as the first contributor to religious freedom. Burgess was also an advocate of the English Separatist descent theory concerning the origin of the General Baptist movement.[32]

Champlin Burrage's work is significant in that he denies that the Separatists in England were influenced by the continental Anabaptist movement. His opinion was that Smyth and Helwys were influenced by English Anabaptism and he even records that perhaps one of these English Anabaptists baptized himself long before Smyth conducted his self-baptism. Burrage, quoting Henoch Clapham's work of 1600, states:

> Touching the Anabaptists, they stand not partaking in the matter (as doth the Brownist) but they exufflate or blow off our Baptisme, so well as Ordination, . . . And so, one baptizeth [From margin: "I know one such, and sundry can witness it."] himselfe (as Abraham

---

29. Choi, "Relationship of John Smyth and Thomas Helwys," 10–11.

30. Burgess, *John Smith the Se-Baptist*.

31. Ibid., 277.

32. Ibid., 66. This theory states that the primary origination of the General Baptist movement began with the Separatists who, true to their name, separated from the Church of England.

first circumcised himselfe: Mary, Abraham had a commandment; they haue none, nor like cause) and then he baptizeth others . . . [33]

This statement, of course, contradicts the Burgess view of English Separatist descent theory for the origin of the General Baptists. Burgess and Burrage defined the two basic views of the origin of the General Baptists but had complete unity in their estimation of Thomas Helwys.

As Burrage reviewed Helwys, he concluded that *A Short Declaration of the Mystery of Iniquity* was a treatise on religious liberty. He stated:

> Helwys appeals to King James I against the Hierarchy of the Reformation, which he interprets to be the second Beast in the Book of Revelation, and asks that his congregation may have freedom to worship by themselves without disturbance from Archbishops, Bishops, and other high officials in the Established Church.[34]

Burrage does not make any new contribution concerning Thomas Helwys's role in the General Baptist movement. He simply continued the pattern of allotting the role of a religious liberty advocate to Helwys.

William T. Whitley provided a newer version of John Smyth's works into modern English. In his *Biography* of John Smyth, Whitley credits John Smyth as being the first to advocate religious freedom and Helwys as the second person to do so. He states:

> Smyth was the first to plead for full religious liberty of conscience. The honour clearly is not due to Browne or Harrison, nor even to Robinson, whose seven articles, sent to the Privy Council in 1617, acknowledge the power of the king to appoint bishops and bestow authority on synods and assemblies. It is equally clear that Helwys in 1612, Busher in 1614, Murton in 1615, were explicit claiming it. But few have noticed that they learned it from Smyth, whose article 84 is most sweeping.[35]

Even though Whitley concluded that Smyth was the first to call for religious liberty, he still assigns Helwys the same role of religious advocate.

---

33. Burrage, *Early English Dissenters*, 223.

34. Ibid., 254.

35. Whitley, *Works of John Smyth*, 1:cxx.

Middle-to-Latter Twentieth Century

In the mid-twentieth century English Baptist historian Barrington R. White produced several works that argue for the English Separatist descent theory. Referring to John Smyth as a Separatist, White states:

> It was to be he who introduced Separatist principles to what he believed to be their logical and Scriptural conclusion when he became convinced that the baptism of believers was the only true Christian baptism in spite of the chorus of shocked horror from his former friends and well as his acknowledged foes.[36]

The argument for Smyth's Separatist lineage underscores the fact that as he taught these principles to his congregation, Helwys embraced these principles and would not soon dismiss them. In effect, Smyth had laid the theological structure that was in place for the leadership of Thomas Helwys. His pastorate maintained the Baptist ecclesiology of Smyth as he took the Baptist congregation back to England.

White comments on Helwys's decision to take the newfound Baptist movement back to England. He writes: "They apparently returned in 1612 and printed, *A Short Declaration of the Mystery of Iniquity*, with an appeal to King James I for toleration of both their beliefs and those of others."[37] In his article, "Early Baptist Arguments for Religious Freedom: Their Overlooked Agenda," White is more pointed regarding Helwys's motive. He states that Helwys wanted "the king to dismantle the whole of the power of the state establishment of the Episcopal church in England . . . what he did desire was that it should lose its powerful, persecuting position in English society."[38] Barry White credits Helwys with understanding that religious liberty in the English society could be implemented only if the king demanded the Church of England to allow religious dissent.

As James Leo Garrett Jr. analyzes the work of Helwys, he states that *A Short Declaration of the Mystery of Iniquity* is "the earliest extant treatise in England advocating religious liberty for all persons."[39] In *Baptist Theology: A Four-Century Study*, Garrett affirms his earlier conclusion, stating that Helwys's work "was a bold advocacy of religious freedom."[40] Garrett goes

---

36. White, *English Separatist Tradition*, 116.

37. White, *English Baptists of the Seventeenth Century*, 22.

38. White, "Early Baptist Arguments for Religious Freedom," 6.

39. Garrett, "Restitution and Dissent Among Early English Baptists: Part II," 23.

40. Garrett, *Baptist Theology*, 33–34.

on to to say that *A Short Declaration of the Mystery of Iniquity* "was a major milestone in the entire struggle for religious liberty."[41]

Leon McBeth wrote the textbook that became the standard for Baptist studies in the latter part of the twentieth century. His work, *The Baptist Heritage: Four Centuries of Baptist Witness*, taught many seminarians the rudiments of Baptist history.[42] In this work, McBeth adheres to the English Separatist descent theory for Baptist origins. As McBeth recapitulates the story of the General English Baptists, he reviews Thomas Helwys's contribution to the movement. He states:

> Soon after their return to England, Helwys published his famous work, *A Short Declaration of the Mystery of Iniquity* (1612). This polemical attack upon the Church of England, and its defense of religious liberty for all, soon got Helwys into trouble. . . . Perhaps the king was offended by the bluntness of Helwys's appeal for religious liberty; at any rate, Helwys was soon in Newgate Prison, where apparently he died in 1616.[43]

Leon McBeth attributes the work of Helwys as being focused upon religious liberty. McBeth does not comment upon the ecclesiology of Helwys nor adds anything new to the General Baptist story. Two noteworthy authors from the mid-twentieth century are James Coggins and William R. Estep. Both men support the Anabaptist kinship theory. This theory stated that "Anabaptism both on the Continent and in England prepared the way for Separatism."[44] In Coggins's book, *John Smyth's Congregation: English Separatism, Mennonite Influence, and the Elect Nation*, he reviews the work of Helwys and states that "Helwys was advocating religious toleration, the separation of church and state."[45]

In William R. Estep's work, *The Anabaptist Story*, he acknowledges that Helwys's book, *A Short Declaration of the Mystery of Iniquity*, was a call for religious liberty. Estep states, "In 1612 an Englishman could read a vigorous plea for complete religious liberty and the separation of church and state. Helwys was the author of this historic statement, the first to be published in English."[46] In another work, Estep makes the claim that "Helwys

---

41. Ibid.
42. McBeth, *Baptist Heritage*.
43. Ibid., 38.
44. Ibid., 52.
45. Coggins, *John Smyth's Congregation*, 130.
46. Estep, *Anabaptist Story*, 224.

advocated complete freedom for all those so categorized and others as well, specifically Roman Catholics, Turks, and Jews."[47] Estep continues his assessment on Helwys as a contributor to religious freedom, stating:

> This book set forth the concept of religious liberty and the institutional separation of church and state. Helwys argued that not only should dissenters have the freedom to worship and to serve the Lord according to their own consciences, but also that Catholics, Jews, Muslims, and pagans were entitled to this same kind of freedom.[48]

Estep concludes that Helwys was the first to plead for religious toleration for all people groups, in spite of their religion.

Summary of the Survey

Each of the historians and theologians covered depicts Thomas Helwys's *A Short Declaration of the Mystery of Iniquity* to have been written to address religious liberty in England. There is no doubt that Helwys wrote to address the persecution of England during the reign of King James I. However, he wrote with a specific point in mind. If he condemned all other ecclesiological options, then logically he was offering Baptist ecclesiology as the most biblical and viable alternative. No one surveyed seems to have considered that the primary purpose of *A Short Declaration of the Mystery of Iniquity* was not limited to advocate religious liberty, but also sets forth the outline of what has become known as Baptist ecclesiology. Malcolm Yarnell did mention the focus of Helwys but did not develop this focus in his work, *The Formation of Christian Doctrine*.[49]

A Short Declaration of the Mystery of Iniquity

Thomas Helwys and the Baptist Church returned to England in order to plant their church on English soil. The rationale for that event was to be a witness to England. Helwys states, "the disciples of Christ cannot glorify God and advance his truth better than by suffering all manner of persecution for it, and by witnessing it against the man of sin, with the blood of

---

47. Estep, "Thomas Helwys," 32.

48. Estep, "Anabaptists, Baptists, and the Free Church Movement," 316.

49. Yarnell, *Formation of Christian Doctrine*, 153.

their testimony."[50] Again, the practical effect of Helwys's position was the desire to advance the Gospel in England. The rationale seems to be that he was convinced that they had restored the true church and he wanted to evangelize England within his ecclesiological and theological framework. Thus, he writes, "so we wish all to do that fear God and seek the glory of his name, and come and lay down their lives in their own country for Christ and his truth."[51]

With the above background establishing the context of *A Short Declaration of the Mystery of Iniquity*, the book evidences that Helwys thought through the ecclesiology of the Baptist position. He structures the book into four parts. The first part (Book One) deals with the first beast or the Church of Rome. Helwys states:

> Who can deny but this is general, eve a general desolation when the saints are overcome, "and when all that dwell, upon the earth (as follows verse 8) shall worship the beast." All our particular knowledge of the fulfilling of this prophecy will make it more evident. And who does not know and see that this prophecy is fulfilled in that Romish mystery of iniquity, "who yet sits upon many waters, with whom have committed fornication the kings of the earth, and the inhabitants of the earth are drunken with the wine of her fornication?" (Rev 17:2).[52]

The rationale for this view is that Roman Catholicism is the mother of all abominations (infant baptism, popes, lack of tolerance to dissenters, etc.), so that if the mother gives birth then the child must also be a beast. With the ground work laid, Helwys continues to examine the second beast. He states:

> Which way now (in finding out the second beast) shall we be able to look beside that great hierarchy of archbishops and lord bishops? Are not you they that pretend (in meekness and humility) the word and power of the Lamb, who says, "Learn of me that I am meek and lowly, etc.," but exercise the power of the beast, speak like the dragon? Have you not made and set up the image of the beast? Is not your pomp and power like his? And has there not been much like cruelty used by that power? Does not the blood of the dead cry? Are not your canon and consistories, and all the power that belongs to them, with all the rest of your courts, offices,

50. Helwys, *Mystery of Iniquity*, 149.

51. Ibid., 154.

52. Ibid., 12.

and officers, are not these part of the image? Are they not like the beast?[53]

Helwys demonstrates that Rome (the first beast) and the Church of England (the second beast) have nothing in common with true Christianity.

Book Two is Helwys's defense of the freedom of conscience. This defense means that he could be considered a heretic by the Church of England and a civil traitor to the nation of England. Yet, in spite of the precarious position, he addresses this section to the king. The basis of this section is that Helwys recognizes the right of the king to govern England. He states:

> Our lord the king has power to take our sons and daughters to do all his services of war and of peace, year, all his servile (civil) services whatsoever. And he has power to take our lands and goods of whatsoever sort or kind, or the tenth thereof to use at his will . . . in all these things our lord the king is to be submitted unto and obeyed. . . . Thus does God give our lord the king power to demand and take what he will of his subjects, and it is to be yielded to him, and to command what ordinance of man he will, and we are to obey it.[54]

Helwys does not deny the right of the king to govern his subjects. In all matters that pertain to civil life, Helwys defends the king's right to govern. The problematic concept is that Helwys understands that the throne is limited to civil matters only. Thus, the king and government do not have the right to govern the church or force religious service upon the subjects.

Book Three rebukes the Puritans who are a part of the Church of England. Basically, he understands that the Puritans are still a part of the second beast and as such they are deemed "false prophets."[55] Helwys's criticism of the Puritans also allowed him to defend Baptist ecclesiology against Presbyterianism. Helwys acknowledges that Christ is the head of the church, thus denouncing any claims otherwise even though the Puritans embrace the leadership of the King of England, Archbishop, and Lords.[56]

Book Four reviews the Separatists and particularly Helwys's former friend, John Robinson. He charges that Separatists are inconsistent in their theological position. They desire to separate from the Church of England but keep their baptism as administered by the church. Thus, he accurately

53. Ibid., 16.
54. Ibid., 33.
55. Ibid., 67.
56. Ibid., 77–80.

accused the Separatists of not actually separating from the Church of England.

This issue provides Helwys the opportunity to discuss the importance of baptism within the framework of ecclesiology. He examines the Separatist covenantal approach to the Scriptures and finds it lacking in substance. He argues, "And whereas he says he will make a new covenant not according to the old, you will say and have it according to the old."[57] Covenantal theology declared that there was a correspondence between the Old Covenant and the New Covenant. Helwys argues against this concept by interpreting the text according to the plain meaning of Scripture.

A Short Declaration of the Mystery of Iniquity includes a call for religious freedom for all dissenting groups, but it goes further. Helwys also makes the point that the Puritans, the Church of England, the Separatists, and the Roman Catholic Church, all miss the meaning of ecclesiology. The reader is left with the impression that Helwys believed that Baptists alone understood the New Testament teachings on the church. The underlying message is that Baptists are not of the false church, but rather the Baptists are the true church.

Methodology

The book will trace the chronology of the events and writings that occurred as revealed from the pen of Thomas Helwys. The chronology of the writings will yield the ecclesiological development of Helwys's thought, which gave rise to the burgeoning General Baptist movement.

The proposed book will interact with the contents of Thomas Helwys's *A Short Declaration of the Mystery of Iniquity*. The methodology will follow Helwys's outline by examining his understanding of Roman Catholicism, the Church of England, Royal Supremacy, Puritanism, and Separatism. This approach will necessitate a chronological review of Helwys's other works such as *A Declaration of Faith of the English People Remaining at Amsterdam*,[58] *A Confession of Faith of the True English Church*,[59] and *An Advertisement or Admonition unto the Congregations, Which Men Call the New Fryelers, in the Lowe Countries*.[60] The relationship between John Smyth and

57. Ibid., 122.
58. Helwys, *Declaration of Faith*, 114–15.
59. Helwys, *Confession of the True English Church*, 57–59.
60. Ibid., 93–154.

Thomas Helwys is critical to understanding Helwys's Baptist ecclesiastical position. Consequently, a review of Smyth's works is crucial.

Chapter Contents

Chapter 1 establishes the context for the book. It expands upon the central theme of Helwys's use of the Book of Revelation to critique Roman Catholicism. Chapter 2 will continue to examine Helwys's use of the Book of Revelation to critique the Church of England and Royal Supremacy. This chapter will argue that Helwys rejected Royal Supremacy over the Church but not over the civil affairs of England.

Chapter 3 will examine Helwys's rationale for condemning Puritanism. His argument against the Puritans was that they still embrace a false ecclesiology. The argument against the Puritans is that their logic falls short of embracing a true ecclesiology. Thus, Helwys begins to depict the fundamental differences between Puritan and Baptist movement. The issue of covenanted church versus of believers' baptism will be explored as to which practice reflects the biblical model for a New Testament church.

Chapter 4 will consider Helwys's argument against royal supremacy. This chapter will examine the rise of relationship of the English Monarchy to the concept of royal supremacy. The lives of Henry VIII, Edward IV, Queen Mary, and Queen Elizabeth will be reviewed. The development of the Church of England will be examined, and a comparison between the national church and Baptist ecclesiology will be considered.

Chapter 5 will review Helwys's arguments against the Puritan movement. The Puritan concept of reform will be considered, along with their meaning of covenant. Their interpretation of covenant will demonstrate that it kept them related to the Church of England in some fashion. Their definition of covenant will also reveal they followed Augustine's meaning of the visible and invisible church as he struggled with the Donatists. The chapter will conclude with a comparison of Puritan church polity with Baptist church polity.

Chapter 6 will examine the Separatist movement and its changing definition of covenant. The book will demonstrate how this new definition allowed the Separatists physically to leave the Church of England. This chapter will review the meaning of a "gathered covenanted church" and demonstrate where Helwys kept the basic formula, but expanded on the meaning of entering into the gathered church. The investigation of believer's baptism will be reviewed to reveal the influence of John Smyth upon Thomas Helwys.

The chronological evaluation of Helwys's writings is to ascertain his growing conviction of Baptist ecclesiology. This evaluation will demonstrate that his work, *A Short Declaration of the Mystery of Iniquity*, was the product of growing conviction that he and the church had embraced a biblical ecclesiology.

2

The English Reformation and Their Understanding of the Book of Revelation

Introduction

ENGLISH PROTESTANTISM WAS ESTABLISHED during the reign of Henry VIII and accompanied with an extensive interpretive apocalypticism. The general mood of the time and the methodology of interpreting current events as being the fulfillment of the Apocalypse had serious overtones of the hideous reign of the Antichrist, the Roman Catholic Church, and the end of the world. The fact that the sixteenth-century Protestant world interpreted current events as signs of eschatological fulfillment of Revelation was indicative of sixteenth-century hermeneutical methodology in that several of the Protestant Reformers (both Magisterial and Radical) believed they were living in the last days as described by Revelation.

The 1535 Münster debacle, along with Martin Luther's insistence that the pope was the Antichrist, demonstrates how widespread the foreboding apocalyptic interpretation had grown in popularity. The issue for apocalyptic methodology was that it was just as much a "mood of the times" as a hermeneutical method.[1] For example, early in his ministry, Luther rejected Revelation for not teaching Christ. Luther wrote:

> I miss more than one thing in this book, and it makes me consider it to be neither apostolic nor prophetic. First and foremost,

1. Bauckham, *Tudor Apocalypse*, 11.

the apostles do not deal with visions, but prophesy in clear and plain words, as do Peter and Paul, and Christ in the gospel . . . . My Spirit cannot accommodate itself to this book. For me this is reason enough not to think highly of it: Christ is neither taught nor known in it.[2]

Even though Luther, in 1522, did not accept Revelation as canonical, he did regard the pope, or at least the Roman Catholic Church, as the Antichrist. In his sermon preached in 1521, "The Misuse of the Mass," he stated:

I myself experience daily how extremely difficult it is to lay aside a conscience of long standing, one that has been fenced in by man-made ordinances. O with how much greater effort and labor, even on the basis of the Holy Scriptures, have I been barely able to justify my own conscience; so that I, one alone, have dared to come forward against the pope, brand him as the Antichrist, the bishops as his apostles, and the universities as his brothels![3]

Apparently, Luther did identify the pope as the Antichrist. The result of this particular assessment is that he believed he was living in the last days.

This sense of doom and his position that the pope was the Antichrist may have led Martin Luther to reassess his position on Revelation. By 1530, Luther abandoned his position that Revelation was outside the canon. Subsequently, this allowed him to embrace a historicist hermeneutical approach that led him to interpret the meaning of John's visions as being congruent with current history. Commenting on Revelation 14 Luther wrote:

Christ first begins to slay his Antichrist with "the breath of his mouth," as St. Paul says [II Thess. 2:8]. The angel with the gospel encounters the bitter scroll of the mighty angel [10:1, 8–10]. The saints and virgins stand again about the Lamb and preach the truth. Upon the gospel follows the second angel's voice, saying that the city of Babylon shall fall [14:8], the spiritual papacy be destroyed. Then follows further that the harvest shall come, and those who cling to the papacy against the gospel shall be cast outside the city of Christ, into the wine press of God's wrath.[4]

Even though Luther assumed he was living in the last days, he now had support via the Book of Revelation. Luther did a cursory review of church history in order to announce that he was not the first to interpret the pope

2. Luther, *Preface to the Revelation of St. John*, 35:398.
3. Luther, *Misuse of the Mass*, 36:398.
4. Luther, *Preface to the Revelation of St. John*, 35:407.

as being the Antichrist.[5] This would give Luther credibility as an exegete in that he would have historical precedence for his conclusions.

In 1530, Luther depicted the mood of apocalypticism as a present reality. Again he wrote:

> Here, now, the devil's final wrath gets to work: there in the East is the second woe, Mohammed and the Saracens; here in the West are papacy and empire, with the third woe . . . Thus, Christendom is plagued most terribly and miserably, everywhere and on all sides, with false doctrines and with wars, with scroll and with sword. That is the dregs, the final plague. After that come almost exclusively images of comfort, telling of the end of all these woes and abominations.[6]

The end result is that, to him, Luther had biblical proof that he was living in the last days, which were depicted in current events that, in his mind, were indicative of the imminence of the end-time.

The Münster problem has been described as one of mood that culminated in horrific events. Irvin Buckwalter Horst comments, "The establishment of the Anabaptist city-state at Münster, in 1534–1535, was an expression of the popular religious feeling generated by the Reformation."[7] Concerning the Münster debacle, a word of clarification is in order. The fiasco seems to be unrepresented by any major movement or theologian. Menno Simons, Dirk Philips, and Dutch Anabaptists, in general, denounced the Münster agenda. In fact, the orientation of their lives to peaceful living, evangelism, and martyrdom is the exact opposite of the Münster motif. Sixteenth-century Anabaptism was more characteristic of pacifism than of violent revolution. For that matter, the typical Anabaptist understood his mandate as being called to suffer and bear the cross, not defend it with violence.[8]

---

5. Ibid., 35:399–411. Luther does not explicitly state that others have interpreted the pope as the Antichrist. However, he does use the apocalyptic method to interpret the book as being fulfilled through past events that took place in church history. He leaves the reader the impression that this interpretive approach was a longstanding tradition.

6. Ibid., 35:407.

7. Horst, *Radical Brethren*, 66.

8. *Schleitheim Confession*, 15. Article 7 rejects the position that a Christian can also be a magistrate based upon the issue that a magistrate was forced to use the sword in defense of the government or in the case of capital punishment.

John Hut demonstrated the eschatological mood, coupled with evangelistic fervor, and accompanied by pacifism during one of his sermons. George Hunston Williams writes:

> It was the fall of 1526 that Hut preached his sermon in condemnation of the peasants for prematurely resorting to the sword in their uprising. In God's time, which Hut thought he could calculate with some precision, the righteous would be given the authority to rule and the ungodly would be overthrown. The Christians in the meantime should flee to Mühlhausen, Nuremberg, and Hungary, awaiting the judgment of God on Christendom through the Turks as the rod of his anger.[9]

The issue of English Apocalypticism does not necessarily trace its origins to Luther or any Magisterial Reformers, nor to the Anabaptists. The social climate of the Reformation saw a general apocalyptic mood prevail but, particularly in England, the popularity of that mood and the subsequent English commentaries on the Antichrist are to be found within English roots.[10] However, to discount the influence of the Anabaptists and the Magisterial Reformers would be most negligent.[11]

The English Apocalyptic Tradition

The English Protestant movement did not begin with John Bale. However, his commentary, *The Image of Both Churches*, was "the first extensive work of apocalyptic interpretation in English Protestantism and the first commentary in English on the Book of Revelation."[12]

---

9. Estep, *Anabaptist Story*, 57.

10. This is not to say that the Magisterial and Radical Reformers did not have an impact in England. They most certainly impacted England with ecclesiological studies, hermeneutical methodology, and evangelistic fervor. The point being made is that England was motivated by its own reformers, which were likely influenced by both Magisterial and Radical branches of the Reformation.

11. Horst and Patterson both argue for a strong Anabaptist presence in London in the early 1500s. See Horst's work cited above. See Patterson, "Genetics Versus Historiography."

12. Bauckham, *Tudor Apocalypse*, 22.

John Bale

John Bale was a friar in Cambridge who converted to Protestantism. He became good friends with Thomas Cromwell, and wrote plays which were designed to present to the audience the teachings of reformed theology and the failure of the Roman Catholic Church. His friend and political leader Cromwell was executed in 1540, which was cause for Bale's exile to continental Europe. During his exile, Bale visited many Protestant cities, allowing him access to libraries and works which were easily available in Continental Europe. Bale undertook the task of writing a commentary on Revelation. He entitled the book, *The Image of Both Churches*.[13] Katherine R. Firth states that Bale wrote the first part of his commentary early in his exile. She writes:

> Early in his exile he wrote the first part of his commentary on the Apocalypse. This first part of his commentary was heavily documented. He read by 1541 the commentaries of Joachim, John Wyclif, Francis Lambert, Sebastian Franck, and Sebastian Myer, to name only a few of the authors cited. He collected together the names of all the authors he could find who had written on the subject, catalogued them by their ecclesiastical order, or by their adherence to Protestantism for the most recent ones, and said he had either seen or read the greater part of the works listed.[14]

Bale makes the claim that he was not the first to write upon the Apocalypse. He opines, "I am not the first which hath attempted this office, or taken upon me this odious enterprise, full of rebukes and slanders; and that maketh me the bolder."[15]

The Image of Both Churches

Bale's desire to write a commentary on Revelation was "to admonish Christ's flock by this present revelation of their perils past, the dangers to come for

---

13. Bale, *Image of Both Churches*.

14. Firth, *Apocalyptic Tradition in Reformation Britain*, 39.

15. Bale, *Image of Both Churches*, 255. For a concise history of the Apocalyptic concept of two churches living in existence but opposed to one another, see Bauckham, *Tudor Apocalypse*. Bauckham traces the ideological concept of two churches in opposition to one another from the medieval era, and it is highly possible that the concept originated with the Donatist movement during the Augustinian era. See ibid., 17.

contempt of the gospel, which now reigneth there above all in the clergy."[16] The fact that Bale utilized current events of his day and interpreted them as being a valid application for his exegesis of Revelation demonstrates the spiritualizing hermeneutic. His appeal to Joachim's *Expositio* meant that Bale "accepted the Joachimist vision of the history of the church as a progression through seven periods, from the death of Christ to the end of the world, each of which was represented by one of the seven seals of the Apocalypse."[17] Thus, the seven churches represented seven church ages which, in turn, are revealed in each of the seven seals. Bale writes, "These openings betoken not only the manifestation of God's truth for seven ages of the world, but also for seven several times, and after seven divers sorts, from Christ's death to the latter end of the world."[18] His interpretation of the seven seals as being seven distinct church ages allowed Bale to depict five of the seals as being previously fulfilled.

Bale's understanding of the sixth seal did not depict a futuristic application. He concluded that the sixth seal was congruent with the world events of his own time:

> Not yet is the pale horse down, nor his iniquity ended, but still he rageth the world over. Still reigneth the antichrists with their hypocrisy and false doctrine, the pope here in Europe, and other not all unlike him in Asia and Africa. But for that Europe is only known unto us, of that will we only define. In naming the pope we mean not his person, but the proud degree or abomination of the papacy. The great Antichrist of Europe is the king of faces, the prince of peace hypocrisy, the man of sin, the father of errors, and the master of lies, the Romish pope.[19]

The significance of this comment is that Bale identified current events as evidence of the end of the world, but he also acknowledged that the office of pope is the Antichrist and not necessarily a person. This is evidence of a spiritualized hermeneutic applied to the text. By doing this, Bale argued that Roman Catholicism is actually a system of the Antichrist, or a persecuting church, which denounces, slanders, or persecutes the true church, meaning the Reformed Church. He demonstrated that the Roman Catholic

---

16. Ibid.
17. Firth, *Apocalyptic Tradition*, 41.
18. Bale, *Image of Both Churches*, 313.
19. Ibid., 325.

Church had become a persecuting church, whereas, the Reformed Church was the persecuted church.

Bale's comment on the sixth seal meant that he not only denied future fulfillment of the passage, but also he understood the text as being applicable to specific events of England and the Reformation in general. An example of this feature was his commentary on the earthquake of Rev 6:2:

> Most lively was this fulfilled such time as William Courtenay the archbishop of Canterbury, with antichrist's synagogue of sorcerers, sat in consistory against Christ's doctrine in John Wicliffe. Mark the year, day, and hour, and ye shall wander at it. . . . Such a terrible earthquake was the general council of Constance against John Huss and Jerome of Prague; and here in England against the King (when he set forth the gospel) the seditious rising of Lincolnshire and the traitorous uproar of Yorkshire in the pilgrimage without grace, whereas neither wanted the false council of bishops, the riches of the abbeys, of benefices, nor yet the cruel hearts of priests.[20]

The irony of Wyclif's trial is that London experienced an actual earthquake on the first day of Wyclif's proceedings. Stephen E. Lahey comments, "That day, London was shaken by a rare and violent earthquake, which terrified several council members."[21]

Bale not only applied the earthquake to current events, but also attributed the fallen stars as being the fall of the Roman Catholic Church. Again he stated:

> And the stars from heaven fell down upon the earth. The ministers of God's word, which should declare his righteousness, and be the lights of the world, were fallen from the heavenly doctrine of Christ and from the sincere scriptures to worldly learning and earthly fantasies. Nothing can be more evident than this, specially to them that have read the trifling works of the sophisters, sententioners, school-doctors, canonists, and summists . . . So that heaven hath vanished away from them, as doth a scroll when it is rolled up together: true preaching of the word, which is very heaven, hath been withdrawn, the verity hath been closed up. Christ hath taken leave, the Spirit of God hath forsaken them, the sincere faith hath failed. . . . Nothing hath remained spiritual, godly, heavenly, holy, righteous, wholesome, nor worthy our Christian vocation, among

---

20. Ibid., 326.

21. Lahey, *John Wyclif*, 26.

their solemn shadow and sacred sorceries. If it hath, it was never yet seen. And that know they full well, which hath unfeignedly received Christ's gospel.[22]

Bale's interpretation presented the position that Roman Catholicism was a viable church in its beginning. Attributing the ceremonies and leaders of the Catholic Church as evidence of their fall allowed Bale to present the Reformed movement as the Lord's true church.

Along with the destruction of the false church, he presented the reign and triumph of the Reformed church in the seventh seal. Bale wrote:

> This signifieth that there shall be in that age that peace in the Christian Church which Christ brought with him from heaven, and left here with his disciples. Then shall the wretched Babylon fall, then shall the bloody beast full of blasphemous names perish, then shall the great antichrist with his whole generation come altogether to nought, then shall the fierce dragon be tied up for a thousand years.[23]

Bale interpreted the seventh seal as ushering in the reign of the true church. This is a future event that can only occur if the dragon (Satan) is bound. This meant Bale took the position that the Antichrist is under the control of Satan. The result is that Bale distinguished between the identity of the Antichrist, which is the office of pope, and Satan who controls the office.

Bale understood that the peaceful reign of the church during the binding of Satan will come to an end once the thousand years are complete. Satan is released to attack the church once again through Gog and Magog. He interpreted Gog to mean the pope and Magog as Islam. Bale claimed that if one were to study the works of Josephus, "Ye well perceive the Holy Ghost to mean none other here by this Gog and Magog, but the Romish pope and Mahomet, with their blasphemous and wicked generations."[24]

The climactic battle between the persecuting church and the persecuted church was ongoing, but Bale depicted the dramatic outcome in decisive favor of the Reformed Church. He depicted that the Romanish pope and Magog will be destroyed, but not annihilated so that they will experience eternal punishment for their deeds. He asserted:

---

22. Bale, *Image of Both Churches*, 329.

23. Ibid., 314.

24. Ibid., 517.

> That word of the Lord's indignation shall with great violence throw the devil, that wily serpent which deceived Gog and Magog with their innumerable soldiers, into a foul stinking lake, or boiling pit of wild fire and brimstone. "Upon the wicked (saith David) shall the Lord rain snares; wild fire, brimstone, with terrible storm and tempest, shall they have their reward," for their eternal punishment. Herein are to be marked and considered both the intolerable grievousness of pains, and also the everlasting continuance of them.[25]

Christ's destruction of Gog and Magog ushers in the Judgment and then the subsequent eternal state of the church worshipping its king.

Contribution of The Image of Both Churches

The fact that Revelation was written by an apostle in exile was not lost on Bishop John Bale. Another notable fact is that the Apostle John wrote it to churches who were suffering or about to suffer persecution. Additionally, the temptation to embrace false doctrine was pointed reason for Bale to write a commentary that had specific application to the English Reformation. As Bauckham observes, "The parallel helped to give a sense of prophetic vocation to English exiles who undertook to address their countrymen in apocalyptic terms. . . . Especially was this true of John Bale, whose exile gave him a sense of identification with St John on Patmos (Rev 1:9)."[26]

Since Bale's work, *The Image of Both Churches*, was the first work to appear in English, it "marked the beginning of original activity in the apocalyptic tradition on the part of English reformers."[27] Bale attempted to demonstrate that the situation in England was nothing less than a conflict between two types of churches, for example, one that had fallen, and one which was reforming that which had fallen. Bale was not necessarily seeking justification for the Reformed Church in England as much as he believed that the events described in Revelation were actually about the Reformation. He purports, "The explicit claim that historical research and apocalyptic exegesis should go closely hand in hand, as necessary partners in the historiographical task, was new."[28]

25. Ibid., 575.
26. Bauckham, *Tudor Apocalypse*, 63–64.
27. Firth, *Apocalyptic Tradition*, 57.
28. Bauckham, *Tudor Apocalypse*, 70.

Thus, Bale's approach to history and exegesis allowed him to place emphasis on events and places as actual prophecies of Revelation, which were fulfilled during the English Reformation. He embraced the idea that Revelation was this history of the Church and, as such, the true church, through persecution, would eventually triumph. This was the moral story Bale wanted Protestant England to learn as recorded in *The Image of Both Churches.*

John Foxe

Bale wrote about the moral and theological character of the two churches, but it was John Foxe who attempted to trace their history. His work, *Acts and Monuments,*[29] depicts the lineage of the true church throughout history. The approach Foxe used was to demonstrate that Bale's contribution has historical validation. He stated:

> For first to see the simple flocke of Christ, especially the vnlearned sort, so miserably abused, and all for ignoraunce of history, not knowing the course of times, and true descent of the Church, it pitied me, that part of diligence so long to haue bene vnsupplyed in this my countrey Church of England. Agayne considering the multitude of Chronicles and storywriters, both in England, and out of England, of whom the most part haue bene either Monkes or clientes to the sea of Rome, it greued me to behold how partially they handled their stories.[30]

Foxe took the position that history, even though available to all, has not been properly handled or recorded accurately. The underlying presupposition is that church history will support the lineage of the true church as it descended from Jesus Christ. Foxe concluded that the fact England did not know about the true church is because the history of the persecuted church was unavailable. He attributed England's lack of knowledge concerning the true church to the Monks' partiality toward Rome, which is proof, for Foxe, that they did not handle the stories correctly or fairly.

29. Foxe, *Unabridged Acts and Monuments.*

30. Foxe, "Preface to Acts and Monuments, 1570." In order to facilitate the flow of the text, making it less tedious for the reader of this book, *sic* will not be used in the frequent occurrences of antiquated language.

Foxe as Historian

Protestant scholars persuaded Foxe to work on a complete history of the English martyrs. This approach meant he would undertake the task of writing on the martyrs throughout English history, concluding his work with the reign of Henry VIII.[31]

A word about Foxe's dating system is in order. Even though he basically agreed with Bale in that the church became apostate in the time of Gregory the Great and the rise of Islam, Foxe declared that a decisive break did not happen until the year AD 1000. He stated:

> Although the church than, as I said, began something to incline before, partly by comming in of Mahomet, partly by comming in of wealth and richesse into the church of Rome: yet the old age of the Church, and those latter times (which times the Apostels prophecy of to be so pearylous and daungerous) most of all began at the ful M. yeares and after, at what time Syluester ii. Pope occupied the seat of Rome An. M.[32]

Aside from the slightly differing dates, Foxe did follow the same approach as Bale. He presented the coming of the Antichrist in the Roman system by using the exegesis of Bale's seven seals. The difference between Bale's commentary and Foxe's history is that Foxe assigned real people as the target of the Antichrist or Roman system.

The bulk of these people were Marian Martyrs of which Foxe devotes Book 5 to the terrible reign of Queen Mary. He titled the book, "The fifth section or Tome of this Ecclesiasticall historie conteynyng the horrible and bloudye tyme of Queene Marye."[33] In this section, he described the acts of Mary toward the Protestants. To cite Queen Mary as part of the Roman system is to arouse the passions of the English people. This was not lost on

31. Firth, *Apocalyptic Tradition*, 81. For a concise review of reformation history scholars working in the sixteenth century, see ibid., chapter 3 entitled, "The Marian Exiles and Foxe's *Acts and Monuments*." Firth examines the role of the continental Protestant scholars as they attempted to collect bibliographies, examine public records, review letters, and generally combine resources in order to write various church histories, historical theology, and commentaries. As both Foxe and Bale were in exile on the continent, they proved to be productive by working out their theology and historiography, which contributed to the English Protestant Reformation. Additionally, Firth writes, "During these years, continental Protestantism enjoyed the facilities of many reformed or newly established academies and universities." Ibid., 69.

32. Foxe, *Acts and Monuments*, 1563 edition, 27; bold in original.

33. Ibid., 957.

Foxe. One such example is the life, ministry, and martyrdom of Laurence Saunders. Foxe chronicled this man's life and presented it as one of great promise. He was arrested for preaching and received the death penalty for sedition simply for preaching without official approval from the crown. While awaiting his death sentence, he wrote a passionate letter to his wife concerning the call and the obligation to preach the sufficiency of Jesus Christ. At the end of the letter, he included a personal admonition:

> Deare wyfe, riches haue I none to leaue behynd me, wherwyth to endowe you after the worldly maner. But that treasure of tastynge how swete Christ is vnto hungry conscyences, wherof I thanke my Christ, I do fele part, and would feale more, that I bequeath vnto you, and to the rest of my beloued in Christ, to retayne the same in sense of heart alwaies. Pray, pray. I am mery, and I trust I shall be mery maugre the teeth of all the Deuils in hell. I vtterly refuse my selfe, and resigne my self vnto my Christ, in whom I know I shalbe strong as he seeth nedeful. Pray, pray, pray. L.S.[34]

This example is indicative of the pattern Foxe employed to demonstrate that both churches and their leadership exist currently and have existed simultaneously for an extended period of time.[35]

The fact that Foxe wrote of Saunders and many others revealed his theological and historiographical methodology. Politically, the persecuting church has the power to harm the true church, which has retained proper theology. Historiographically, Foxe recorded such events to demonstrate his point (and Bale's), for instance, that two churches are in existence. One church has a true image with Jesus Christ as its headship, whereas, the other church has a false image and an Antichrist system as its headship. The true church will follow the example of its head and suffer as Christ suffered in juxtaposition to the false church, which will follow its head and reign politically just as the Antichrist rules.

Another issue not to be overlooked is the fact that Foxe took a universal approach to the existence of both churches. In other words, he did not limit them geographically to one event, one place, or even one country. This should be given considerable weight in regard to the role of *Acts and Monuments* in relation to English nationalism. Foxe did not treat England,

---

34. Ibid., 1113.

35. The above example is used to demonstrate that two specific English churches were engaged in mutual conflict. The Roman Church persecuted the clergy of the English Church. This is but one example utilized by Foxe in his work.

as a nation, as an elect nation to serve God's purpose on a national scale. Bauckham correctly states, "that in the context of the universal dimensions of biblical apocalyptic the sufferings and triumphs of the faithful in England could be understood in terms of God's purpose in the world."[36]

However, to conclude that English nationalism was not aided by Foxe would be a misnomer. Firth states the general premise that, "What had been propaganda in the days of Mary easily became apology in the days of Elizabeth."[37] Christopher Hill acknowledges the popularity of Foxe's *Acts and Monuments* during the reign of Elizabeth. He states:

> Foxe's great *Acts and Monuments*, given the widest possible circulation through its use as propaganda by the Elizabethan government, depicted Englishmen throughout the centuries battling against Antichrist, especially since the days of Wyclif . . . Foxe made his countrymen conscious of a long historical tradition, which in itself appeared to legitimate their views, and to confirm their conviction that the corruptions of the papacy were of long standing.[38]

Even though *Acts and Monuments* was used to promote English nationalism, that was not the purpose for the writing of the work.

As stated previously, the fundamental belief was that the office of the pope as the Antichrist was firmly cemented in the Reformation mindset. Foxe added a historical component to that particular belief system. Barbara Griswold comments, "It was the application of the apocalyptic books of Daniel and Revelation that formed the basis of their identification of the Church of Rome as Antichrist, and the papacy of Babylon. It was on this basis that England had justified its separation from Rome."[39] The historical component was present to be used as evidence to advance the Reformed movement, which happened to aid the royal throne of England.

Acts and Monuments and Revelation.

The first edition of *Acts and Monuments* was released in 1563. Three more editions were published in 1570, 1576, and 1583. The revisions of the book illustrate Foxe's growing interest in the apocalyptic interpretive method.

36. Bauckham, *Tudor Apocalypse*, 87.

37. Firth, *Apocalyptic Tradition*, 85–86.

38. Hill, *Antichrist in the Seventeenth-Century England*, 14.

39. Griswold, "Congregational Dynamics," 37.

The preface to the 1570 edition displays Foxe's penchant for the numerical calculation of the biblical text with current events. He attempted to demonstrate that the Babylonian captivity started in 1501 and would end in 1570 or possibly 1576. Foxe wrote:

> And now by reuolution of yeares we are come from that tyme of 1501 to the yeare now present 1570. In which the full seuenty yeares of the Babilonicall captiuitie draweth now well to an end, if we count from the first appearyng of these bloudy markes aboue mentioned. Or if we recken from the beginnyng of Luther, and his persecution, then lacketh yet xvj. yeares.[40]

Even though Foxe was inexact in his calculations, he remained convinced that the end of the world via the Lord's coming was imminent. Bauckham states, "Clearly Foxe right up to the time of his death expected the Lord's coming at any time. He seems to have been untroubled by the inexactitude of his calculations, which functioned only as general hints that history was approaching its End."[41] The difference of the sixteen years and the dating of Luther are significant in that the date of the Reformed movement was firmly established within the English mindset.

The timeframe for the events of the Revelation has been depicted within a threefold division, which is Foxe's method. Richard Bauckham demonstrates this practice:

> Among the various patters which Foxe's apocalyptic exegesis discovered in church history, we have noticed the special prominence of one threefold division which appeared in the Book of Martyrs ... (1) The period of persecution under the pagan Emperors, lasting 294 years and comprising the traditional ten persecutions, (2) The millenium, established by Constantine and ending with the loosing of Satan at the time of the persecution of Wyclif, (3) The second period of persecution, under Antichrist. This too comprised ten persecutions and might also last 294 years. In any case it would end soon and its end would be the Second Coming and the Last Judgment.[42]

Foxe determined that the millennial age has already passed. Bauckham has critiqued Foxe for not having an adequate millennial system. The rationale for this critique is the placement of the millennial reign by Foxe.

---

40. Foxe, *Acts and Monuments*, 1570 ed., 6.

41. Bauckham, *Tudor Apocalypse*, 162.

42. Ibid., 221–22.

Bauckham denies this reign simply because per Revelation 20, Satan is bound and cannot deceive the nations. Bauckham's argument is that Islam did, in fact, deceive the nations. However, Bauckham is willing to concede that Foxe was attempting to unite the Reformation with the Constantinian church as having peace from her persecution.[43] Foxe upheld Constantine as the messenger who brought peace to the church.

Contribution of Acts and Monuments

The impact of *Acts and Monuments* on the English Reformation is considerable. For the first time in the English Reformation, the Reformed Church had a history to validate its position. Couple this with the fact that the Reformed movement now had a reason to oppose Rome, as the fallen church was governed by the Antichrist via the office of the pope. Foxe's work provided a legitimate theological and historical rationale for the Reform movement to exist. In other words, in Foxe's work, the English Reformation now had reasons to leave Rome aside from the divorce of Henry VIII.[44]

In *Acts and Monuments*, Foxe defined the English Reformation. More than that though, he helped establish and explain the academic standard of church historiography. For that matter, he worked with recorded history to seek biblical meaning for current changes within the seventeenth-century world. Firth states, "Foxe was the first British author to write a Protestant apocalyptic history that attempted to explain change in time in terms of unfolding pattern of events."[45]

Helwys's Role Within the English Apocalyptic Tradition

The *Short Declaration of the Mystery of Iniquity* does use the same imagery common to the apocalyptic literature of the previous decades. The direct influence of the book may have been Helwys's father who wrote *A Marvel*

43. In fairness to Bauckham, he does not explicitly word his statement in the fashion in which this writer presents the comparison. However, he does state, "Were there not in fact important aspects of the Reformation period which had more in common with the Constantinian than the pre-Constantinian age?" See Bauckham, *Tudor Apocalypse*, 223.

44. Cross and Livingston, *Oxford Dictionary of the Christian Church*, s.v. "Reformation."

45. Firth, *Apocalyptic Tradition*, 110.

Deciphered.[46] Burgess describes this work as: "A topical patriotic tract called forth by Protestant feeling engendered by the Spanish attack on England. The writer makes a veiled allusion to Queen Elizabeth as foreshadowed by the woman clothed with the Sun in the 12th chapter of Revelation and to the Pope as the Dragon that made war on her."[47] No direct proof exists for the influence of Helwys's father or that their writing styles were similar, but the indirect proof of their relationship does suggest that Thomas Helwys, like his father, stands in the mainstream of apocalyptic genre.

Another indirect proof is the title itself. *The Mystery of Iniquity* is found in Paul's phrase, "the mystery of iniquity is already at work" (2 Thess 2:7).[48] This verse describes the activities of the Antichrist. Helwys picked up on the theme of iniquity at work and applied it to the lack of religious toleration within England. The Church of England was simply intolerant of other religions.

A third consideration is the internal evidence of language Helwys utilized in *Mystery of Iniquity*. For example, he equated the phrase "mystery of iniquity" with Roman Catholicism. Helwys wrote:

> Yet this much have we gained toward the cause in hand, that it being proved that the mystery of iniquity, and the abomination of desolation is exalted to the highest in that Romish profession. And so are all these prophecies fulfilled in our eyes, which have been produced to prove that there has been an utter desolation of Christ's power and authority, and the power and authority of the man of sin exalted.[49]

Like Bale and Foxe, Helwys applied the current religious situation of England as being described within the contents of Revelation. He is even more specific as he interpreted the first beast of Revelation 13 to be Roman Catholicism. Joe Early Jr. has demonstrated that, unlike Bale and Foxe, Helwys hesitated to say that the pope is the Antichrist, but Helwys did make specific points regarding the identities of both. Early writes:

> Though Helwys does not explicitly state it, he implies that the pope is the "man of sin" as noted in 2 Corinthians 6:15–16. If the pope is the man of sin, then it is impossible for Christ to be head

---

46. This book is no longer in existence, and thus no bibliographic material is available.

47. Burgess, *John Smith the Se-Baptist*, 110.

48. 2 Thess 2:7.

49. Helwys, *Mystery of Iniquity*, 14.

of the Roman Catholic Church. Helwys noted that "the man of sin cannot sit with God as God, in the temple." If the pope claims to be the spiritual head of the church, then Christ cannot be, because God does not share his throne.[50]

However, the second beast is interpreted to be the Church of England. Helwys interpreted the actions of the Church of England as being indicative of the first beast. In other words, the official Church of England acted like the official Church of Roman Catholicism. Helwys addressed the Church of England with personal pronouns. He wrote:

> Have you not made and set up the image of the beast? Is not your pomp and power like his? And has there not been much like cruelty used by that power? Does not the blood of the dead cry? And have not the imprisoned groaned under that cruelty? And do not the silenced at home, and the banished abroad daily complain? May not all these cry, "How long, Lord how long? When will you revenge?" Are not your canons and consistories, and all the power that belongs to them, with all the rest of your courts, offices, and officers, are not these part of the image? Are they not like the beast?[51]

Helwys applied Revelation to the Church of England, which was something Bale and Foxe never did. In Helwys's thought, this type of application, for instance, the English church and its current events, were described by the Apocalypse. Even though Bale and Foxe never interpreted Revelation as applicable to the Church of England, Helwys's approach stands in the same tradition of the English Apocalyptic genre of Bale and Foxe.

The approach that Helwys took with the Puritans is that they were the false prophets of the beast. Helwys wrote that Puritans were false prophets, because they taught "many false doctrines."[52] The rationale for Helwys labeling the Puritans as false prophets was that they would not leave the corrupt Church of England. He even stated that by remaining with the Church of England, they "destroy all people that submit to your ministry in that you bring them therein under the power of the beast, you having fallen down on your knees and worshipped the beast, receiving your spirit and office

---

50. Early, "The Apocalyptic Nature of Thomas Helwys's Writings," 457–58.

51. Helwys, *Mystery of Iniquity*, 16.

52. Ibid., 65.

from the beast."[53] Thus, in Helwys's mind, the second beast was using the false prophets; for example, the Puritans to deceive the people of England.

The above examples reveal that Helwys used the same hermeneutical approach as Foxe. He not only used the same hermeneutic, but also continued in the apocalyptic genre and worked with the same methodology as previous generations. However, Helwys extended the interpretation to include the Church of England and English current events to denounce those who still remained part of the English national church.

One last circumstantial evidence as to how Helwys utilized the apocalyptic tradition in his work, *A Short Declaration of the Mystery of Iniquity*, was his decision to return to England. Helwys did believe he was living in the latter times or he could not have interpreted Revelation as being fulfilled in England. Based upon that general conclusion, it was only logical that Helwys felt a sense of urgency to return to England in order to preach the Gospel. Helwys even stated that the best way to present the Gospel was to suffer for it: "For the disciples of Christ cannot glorify God and advance his truth better than by suffering all manner of persecution for it, and by witnessing it against the man of sin, with the blood of their testimony."[54]

Helwys wrote the book to inspire the English Baptist church in Amsterdam to return to England and perhaps face severe persecution. Joe Early Jr. claims that the book was written in Holland and published there in late 1611, prior to the return to English soil.[55] If Early is correct, then it is safe to assume that the book may also have been written for the fledging church to prepare for persecution from their fellow Englishmen. Malcolm Yarnell comments on this theme when he writes that "General Baptists reveal their passion to preach the gospel of Jesus Christ. They were driven by their belief that the teaching of the Word must precede conversion, which must be followed by believer's baptism."[56] Regardless of the actual recipients, the book was born out of a sense of obligation to return to England and initiate change via proclamation of the Gospel.

---

53. Ibid., 69.

54. Ibid., 152.

55. Helwys, *Life and Writings of Thomas Helwys*, 36.

56. Yarnell, "We Believe with the Heart," 19.

3

Helwys's Interpretation of Revelation and the First and Second Beast

His Rationale for Rejecting Roman Catholicism and the Church Of England

Introduction

IN BOOK ONE OF *Mystery of Iniquity*, Helwys referred to the circumstances of Jeremiah the Prophet as he addressed the overthrow of Jerusalem. The destruction of the city, as recorded by Jeremiah, formed the background for the attitude conveyed by Helwys. Like Jeremiah, Helwys was deeply sorrowed and troubled by his current situation. Helwys understood that the people of Jeremiah's day did not understand the issue at hand simply because they would not listen to the prophet's message. To underscore this point, Helwys quoted Jeremiah 37:2.

Helwys then revealed that the message of the prophet was accepted, but only after the fact that the prophecy had been fulfilled. He quoted Lamentations 2:10 to support his position. This verse depicts the "elders of the daughter of Zion" in deep remorse over the destruction of Jerusalem as prophesied by Jeremiah. The point Helwys makes is that the nation of Israel did not even regard much less mourn over the prophecy until it was too late.

The application of Jeremiah's lamentation is that, in the current situation in England, no one seemed to be alarmed that there was just cause for sorrow. Helwys stated:

> And if it cannot be denied but that the hearing and seeing of this prophecy of so great desolation fulfilled was just cause of this great sorrow, where are then the eyes and ears of men that they might hear and see far greater tribulations and desolations than these, prophesied by a greater prophet than Jeremiah, and even now fulfilled in the fierce wrath of judgment by the Most High, and that in the sight of all men? And yet who considers of it? Who takes up lamentation for it? Are men utterly void of mourning affections? Or are they destitute of understanding in the cause of sorrow? Or do men think the danger is past?[1]

Helwys contributed that lack of mourning of the current situation was due to the fact that: (1) men did not understand the prophecy, or (2) they thought the danger of the prophecy by the prophet greater than Jeremiah was already fulfilled.

Helwys demonstrated that the cause for mourning was found in Matthew 24:4–28 and the parallel passage of Luke 21:8–31. These passages referred to Daniel's prophecy of the Abomination of Desolation. The Matthew and Luke passages were categorized by Thomas Helwys as prophecy, and thus the greater prophet's identity was Jesus Christ. Helwys began to demonstrate that Daniel's prophecy of desolations had not been fulfilled in the past, but was currently being fulfilled in the present. He stated:

> Has the like prophecy ever been heard of? Or can there be any desolation like to this desolation, wherein no flesh shall be saved? No, from the beginning of the world there has not been like, nor shall be, says our Savior Christ. Who can remain ignorant of these days and times, and what ignorance is it not to know that these are even the days and times prophesied of?[2]

As quoted by Jesus, the prophecy of Daniel became the platform for writing and warning England that the abomination of desolation was currently being fulfilled through the situation that existed in Reformation England.

---

1. Helwys, *Mystery of Iniquity*, 5.

2. Ibid., 6.

An Ecclesiological Evaluation of Roman Catholicism

Helwys depicted the Roman Catholic Church as the first beast of Revelation 13:1. The beast is that entity which had been given power to speak blasphemies against God. Per Revelation 13:7, the beast had the ability to make war with the saints. Helwys stated, "who can deny but this is general, even a general desolation when the Saints are overcome . . . And who does not know and see that this prophecy is fulfilled in that Romish mystery of iniquity."[3] One of the primary reasons that Helwys denounced the Roman Catholic Church was for their "strange exaltation of power and pomp" that had established the office of pope and bishop.[4]

Helwys not only depicted the pope as powerful, but also as unscriptural and evil. He connected the office of pope with the man of sin in 2 Thessalonians 2:4, 8, when he wrote that "man of sin sits and rules in the church of Christ."[5] Characterized as the man of sin, the pope has become a spiritual power by having "kings and princes bowing to him, and serving him, and (by virtue of his office) carrying a bloody sword, and his hands full of blood . . . taking upon him to have the power to cast soul and body to hell, and to send to heaven whom he will."[6]

The rationale for Helwys's statement was that the beast destroyed the two witnesses of Revelation 11. Working with the rubric of Daniel 9, and the key concept of the abomination of desolation, the timeframe of the events became significant for Helwys. The three and a half years of the Tribulation were at hand, and Helwys based his conclusion that Daniel 9:27's reference to the cessation of the sacrifice and oblations was actually in agreement with Revelation 11. The cessation of the two witnesses was pivotal to Helwys's interpretation of Roman Catholicism. He stated that the two witnesses were revealed in John 15:26 and Acts 5:32 as being "the Spirit of Truth and the Word of Truth."[7]

Helwys supported this conclusion with Revelation 12:14, which alluded to the woman hiding in the wilderness that he interprets to be "kingdom of Christ."[8] Helwys stated:

3. Ibid., 12.
4. Ibid.
5. Ibid., 10.
6. Ibid., 12–13.
7. Ibid., 9.
8. Ibid.

> And in Revelation 12 the woman, which is the kingdom of Christ, the heavenly Jerusalem, the mother of all the faithful (Galatians 4), flees into the wilderness for a time, times and half a time, . . . The true sacrifices, and oblations of the people of God, the Word and Spirit, and the heavenly Jerusalem, the spouse of Christ, ceasing, lying dead in the streets, and being fled into the wilderness, it must needs follow that there was an utter desolation of all the holy things and all the means of salvation.[9]

The two witnesses have ceased to function within this interpretive framework. The Word and Spirit no longer have a ministry within the confines of the Roman Catholic Church. The conclusion was that a true church would have the Word and the Spirit, but since Rome did not possess them, they could not function as a true church. Helwys continued to say the Word and the Spirit were taken from the saints so that the Scriptures could not be translated "into their own language," but that the pope would "deliver it to them and that must stand for the Word and Spirit of God without trying."[10]

This application of prophecy would explain the rationale of Helwys, which stated that the souls of the Roman Catholic Church were perishing. He wrote:

> Yet who can but with compassionate hearts lament to see so many souls perish daily and continually under this destruction? For all the souls upon the earth that exalt, give power, and submit themselves to this man of sin, and so die, they perish to everlasting destruction, although they do it ignorantly. . . . Now, men are deceived by being ignorant of the deceit. And they that are thus deceived through ignorance are they that perish. . . . Here is no exception, ignorant or not ignorant. If they come not forth at the voice of the Lord's call, but still remain and abide there, they shall surely be partaker of her plagues. . . .[11]

The fact that the Scriptures were unavailable to the masses of the Roman Catholic Church was verification, in Helwys's mind, that the people were perishing under the authority of an ungodly system of religion. The fact that the people might or might not be ignorant did not change the fate of the dying soul. Thus, Helwys felt the need to address the situation for the sake of those who were spiritually dying by deceit.

9. Ibid., 9–10.
10. Ibid., 15.
11. Ibid., 13–14.

The Church of Rome as a Deficient Ecclesiology

Based upon the ecclesiology of the Roman Church, Helwys labeled it the first beast found in Revelation 13. In keeping with the nature of apocalyptic literature, the Beast was the antithesis of a godly church. The Beast devoured the Word and Spirit, and then turned its venom on the destruction of the Saints.

The leadership of the Roman Church had replaced the headship of Christ with a Popish system that perpetuated itself. Helwys stated that the ecclesiastical Roman system undermined and even replaced "the whole power of Christ" and abolished the Lord's reign in the church.[12] Therefore, the true church had no choice but to flee into hiding at the reign of the man of sin. The Catholic Church replaced the headship of Christ with the man of sin which now exalted himself above God. For Helwys, the ecclesiastical system is deficient in that the leadership was sinful and ungodly. Furthermore, the actions of the popish system had replaced the Word and Spirit with unscriptural ceremonies. Thus, the conclusion was that the Roman Catholic Church was not a viable option for a true ecclesiology, nor was its ecclesiological offspring known as the second beast.

An Ecclesiological Evaluation of the Church of England

Helwys's interpretation of Revelation 13:11 allowed him to introduce the second beast with the prospect of identifying the ecclesiastical representation as the Church of England. Helwys stated that the characteristics of the second beast had a "great hierarchy of archbishops and lord bishops."[13] This thinly veiled hint was coupled with the description of the actions of the second beast. Helwys declared that the second beast acted in accordance with the first beast as he wrote:

> Are not you they that pretend (in meekness and humility) the word and power of the Lamb, who says, Learn of me that I am meek and lowly, etc., but exercise the power of the beast, and speak like the dragon? Have you not made and set up the image of the

---

12. Ibid., 15.

13. Ibid.

beast? Is not your pomp and power like his? And has there not
been much cruelty used by that power?[14]

Even though the Church of England was never identified by name, the word
"you" and the comparison of the ceremonies to the first beast identified the
official English Church as Helwys's target.

The identity of the Church of England continued as Helwys wrote
that there are those who are "silenced at home" and "the banished abroad
daily complain."[15] The key to understanding the Church of England as
being the second beast was Helwys's identification with his homeland.
Helwys referenced those who were silenced by the laws of England and
those who were banished from England. Further identification was given
when he wrote that "blood of the dead cry" and "the imprisoned groaned
under that cruelty."[16]

Helwys continued to identify the Church of England by comparing
it to Roman Catholicism. He stated that English Church authorities were
like the first image of the beast. "Are not your canons and consistories, and
all the power that belongs to them, with all the rest of your courts, offices,
and officers, are not these parts of the image? Are they not like the beast?"[17]
The identification of the Church of England with the second beast was to
advance the argument that the Church of England is not far removed from
the first beast.

The English national church persecuted the subjects of England by
enforcing conformity to the church. "And do you not all these things, when
you force and compel men to submit to your whole conformity, which is
the perfect image of the beast? Not to speak of your surplice, and cross,
and churchings, and burials and coops, and chantings, and organs in your
cathedrals."[18] The forced worship that England forced upon its subjects
was indicative of the first beast. The second beast acted like its Roman
predecessor.

14. Ibid.

15. Ibid.

16. Ibid.

17. Ibid.

18. Ibid., 17. Greaves interprets the word *coops* to mean *prison*.

Common Book

The issue of prescribed Liturgy enforced by the Church of England allowed Helwys to prove his point by referencing the *Common Book*[19] as used by the Anglican priestly hierarchy. He states:

> By what power do you make prayers and bind men to them, and appoint the order of them in time and place, whereof two you appoint to be read every evening without alteration, some prayers to be said after the curate be paid his due, some on the north side of the table, some in one place, some in another?[20]

The reference to the *Common Prayer Book* as binding was proof of the Church of England compelling worship. Helwys continued to denounce the Anglican-forced worship practice. He continued:

> Will you see a special ground of these four abominations in appointing your priests what to pray, when to pray, and where to pray, and what to put on when they pray, because you made so many priest, and have so many yet among you, as neither know what to pray, where, nor when to pray, nor what to put on when they pray, insomuch as if you did not allow them a sum of made prayers, they had been, and yet would be, altogether without prayers?[21]

The point Helwys makes is that the *Common Book* was the substance of the spiritual depth of the Anglican Church, which was deficient theologically. Without such proactive steps, he was persuaded that the typical parish priest would not have the knowledge of how to pray, when to pray, what to pray, or even what to wear when praying.

Helwys then made the point that if the *Common Book* were to be taken from the Anglican clergy that they would have no spiritual and theological acumen. He wrote:

19. The typical name is the *Book of Common Prayer*. Helwys used the shorter name *Common Book*.

20. Helwys, *Mystery of Iniquity*, 17.

21. Ibid. A word concerning the *English Book of Prayer* may yield insight into the depiction of the Anglican ministry as commented upon by Thomas Helwys. In 1549, the usage of the *Common Book* was mandated by Edward VI. The Book was translated from Latin to English and contained the requirements for Liturgy, Prayers, and Communion. It also contained the required service format for morning and evening prayers, baptisms, marriages, and funerals.

> For take your *Common Book* from them, and then would the im-
> pudent be ashamed of such ministry. Oh, that ten of the best and
> chief of a thousand of those your priests might be debarred from
> your book, and be set in a congregation of very partial hearers of
> their side to show their abilities for the office of the ministry . . . but
> your priests' fault would be found in themselves in that they would
> have no one word to speak to God's glory, nor to edification.[22]

Helwys denounced the Anglican priests as being deficient in content and
not having enough knowledge to function as priests were the *Common
Book* taken from them. This was evidence for Helwys that the Church of
England should have "devised men's prayers, and devise men's repentances,
and they must say and repent as you by your power you appoint them."[23]
Without the *Common Book*, the priests were incapable of performing the
basic ministries required to sustain worship. Benjamin Evans stated that
the priests "had neither good learning nor good name, but were drunkards
and of filthy life."[24]

Titles and Blasphemy

By his review of the titles of the priesthood, Helwys continued to demonstrate that the Church of England was the second beast. He denounced
them as blasphemous. Helwys wrote:

> Lastly, to make it appear plainly enough that this hierarchy of
> archbishops and lord bishops is the image of the beast, let all be-
> hold the names of blasphemy which it bears, and they are these, so
> far as we know the number of them: Archbishops, Primates, Met-
> ropolitans, Lords Spiritual, Reverend Father, Lords Grace. What
> names of blasphemy are here. They are the titles and names of our
> God, and of our Christ.[25]

The issue at hand was that the hierarchy of the Church of England had
taken names that referenced the authority of Christ.

Helwys denounced the clergy for taking the name "Reverend," as this
action and title was an expression of self-exaltation above the congregation.

22. Ibid., 17.

23. Ibid., 18.

24. Evans, *Early English Baptists*, 1:143. I am indebted to Griswold, "Congregational
Dynamics." She revealed Evans's quote on p. 25 of her dissertation.

25. Helwys, *Mystery of Iniquity*, 21.

He quoted Matthew 23:9–11 to support his claim. He wrote, "Are you not exalted above your brethren by this name. Then you are they of whom Christ speaks of in this place, and whom he will bring fallow for thus taking upon you the name of God, and exalting yourselves above the brethren."[26]

Another name Helwys commented on was the name "Lord's Grace." He called this a "household title."[27] He basically stated that this title should only belong to the "Lord of Grace."[28] Helwys took the position that only God can have authority in the church as He is the one who gives grace.

The purpose of reviewing the names and titles of the Anglican clergy was that Helwys connected the Anglican priesthood with the reign of the man of sin, which "will have a kingdom where there shall be mighty power and authority one over another's conscience, appointing and compelling men how they shall worship their God, and to imprison, to banish, and to cause to die them that resist."[29] Helwys actually described the actions of the Anglican Church as many English citizens and subjects resisted and died for their alleged rebellion to the Church of England. Two examples of resistance that resulted in death, and which occurred within a reasonable date of Helwys's writings, are that of Henry Barrow and John Greenwood.

Barrow and Greenwood resisted the Church of England on Separatist grounds. They claimed that the Anglican Church was a false church. Barry White comments that they were passive resisters, but regardless of their position of resistance "Barrow and Greenwood were hanged in April 1593."[30] Since he did not refer to it, no proof exists that this situation was on Helwys's mind as he wrote this section of *Mystery of Iniquity*. However, it was a well-known ecclesiastical-political case that described the conditions on England.

Helwys continued on to say that "the man of sin will have in his kingdom names of most high honor, yea, even the names, titles and attributes of God, and thus does he sit as God in name, title, and power."[31] Helwys was convinced that the prophecy that was declared in Revelation applied to the

---

26. Ibid., 22.

27. Ibid.

28. Ibid., 23.

29. Ibid.

30. White, *English Puritan Tradition*, 89. White goes into much detail concerning the rationale of Barrow and Greenwood for their Separatism.

31. Helwys, *Mystery of Iniquity*, 23.

Church of England. Thus, the titles are nothing more than evidence that the second beast was conceived in the bowels of the first beast.[32]

Imagery of the Beast

Helwys continued his evaluation and subsequent denunciation of the Church of England by referencing Revelation 13:12. The passage stated that the second beast caused the entire earth to worship the first beast. In Helwys's prophetic-ecclesiological paradigm, the first beast was none other than Roman Catholicism. Yet, Helwys did not apply this verse to the English National Church. He wrote:

> Where it is spoken that the second beast causes the earth and them that dwell therein to worship the first beast, and therefore the Romish beast being the first, this hierarchy cannot be the second, in that it does not cause men to worship the pope of Rome, we pray it may be observed how it is showed (2 Thessalonians 2:7, 9, 10) that the mystery of iniquity is a working power of Satan.[33]

Helwys articulated that the second beast did cause all to worship Rome, but now he denied a literal application of the Church of England being the beast which led worship back to Rome. He had been applying the second-beast motif as being the embodiment of the Church of England in a spiritual sense. Helwys started the work with that premise. He wrote: "A main and general reason all this is because this prophecy is of spiritual desolations, destructions and woes, and cannot be understood but with spiritual hearts, nor seen but with spiritual eyes. And the hearts and eyes of men are natural and carnal, and therefore these things cannot affect them (1 Corinthians 2:14)."[34]

Helwys closed the first chapter with the reaffirmation that understanding the prophecy of Revelation is not for those who are carnally minded. Again Helwys stated: "And he did wonders (speaking of the beast) so that he made fire come down from heaven in the sight of men, (Revelation 13:13) and to see how it is fulfilled in the second beast, we must remember (as we formerly said) that this is a spiritual prophecy of a spiritual mystery of iniquity, which none may deny."[35] The specific issue that Helwys attempted

32. Ibid., 24.
33. Ibid., 26.
34. Ibid., 8.
35. Ibid., 27.

to communicate was the spiritual nature of the prophecy. According to Helwys, the prophecy was for mature Christians and the second beast was simply an imagery of the Roman Catholic Church.

Helwys's Use of Counterfactuals

Helwys proved his point by a cursory review of specific counterfactual circumstances. He first recalled that the power of Satan does work throughout the Book of Revelation. There is no question about this fact. The manner in which Satan works is by deception. Helwys stated that Satan's intention is to establish the man of sin with two powers that bring all people to the same conclusion. He stated that "the height of the exaltation thereof, this power is set forth and described to us under the two names and similitudes of the first and second beast."[36] This leads the reader to the conclusion that a similitude is not the actual manifestation of that which it represents. In this case, the second beast represents the first beast, but in and of itself the second beast is not a reality but only a representative of that first. Both beasts have one and the same purpose, which is to bring worship to the first beast. Helwys termed this goal as "one power building up one kingdom."[37]

Utilizing spiritual application, Helwys denied that the literal application of Scripture was the norm for the prophecy. To prove his point, he referred to the first counterfactual of the pope's personhood. If the pope were the man of sin, then the Lord "should abolish and consume the pope's person, but there is no such prophecy of scripture."[38] The Lord could destroy the pope and the man of sin if they were one and the same. Helwys denied this could happen simply because the Scriptures do not reveal this possibility to be true.

The second counterfactual Helwys considered was the destruction of Babylon as a literal fulfillment. He denied the actual destruction of Rome. Helwys wrote:

> And then should the prophecies of the fall of Babylon be understood of the overthrow and consuming of the earthen or stone walls, and timber houses of a city. But this were too carnal an understanding, to conceive that the Spirit of God's mouth which shall consume the man of sin, spoken of 2 Thessalonians 2, and

36. Ibid., 26.
37. Ibid.
38. Ibid.

shall shake asunder the city, which spiritually is called Sodom and Egypt. It were too carnal to understand this to be of earthly houses and cities, and fleshly persons.[39]

The point Helwys made is that Rome or Babylon was not going to be consumed in a literal fashion. The Lord will abolish the man of sin, Babylon, but not literally. The Lord's destruction will abolish the false religions, "but will easily appear to the wise, though some have been, and are, much mistaken herein."[40]

Helwys argued that the dire circumstances of England were spiritual in nature. The English people had embraced a false religion, which Helwys characterized as false fire.[41] The false fire of religion was nothing other than satanic activity working "effectually upon the hearts and affections of those that receive not the love of truth, . . . so that men are strongly persuaded and believe that it is the true fire from heaven, even the Spirit of God."[42] Thus, the English people were deceived by Satan, but they did not know it. Helwys inadvertently attributed this lack of knowledge to their spiritual immaturity.

False Fire and the Hierarchy.

The false fire that deceived the hearts of men manifested itself in the Church of England. "This fire has the hierarchy of archbishops and lord bishops made come down from heaven, . . . with their prayer book, and all their cathedral abominations in such admiration."[43] The reference was that Satan was at work in the inner working of the Anglican Church. The issue of fire denoted that the English Church possessed widespread appeal as the official church. However, this favor of the people would not withstand the judgment of God.

Helwys concluded chapter 1 with the appeal that the membership within the Church of England must consider that the church itself was under divine judgment. He carefully expounded Matthew, Paul, and John's eschatological passages. Helwys's point was to demonstrate biblically that

39. Ibid., 26–27.
40. Ibid., 27.
41. Ibid.
42. Ibid.
43. Ibid.

God's judgment and wrath had already started even though the English Church was unaware. Helwys proved his point by recalling the decline of the Anglican Church. He stated:

> And does not the beauty of the image fade? Is not the baptizing of midwives quite vanished? And does not the bishoping of young and old much decay? Does not the dully reading of injunctions and homilies grow to forgetfulness? And are not profane perambulations laid aside? And do not holy evens and days, and ember weeks almost pass out of mind? And is not the book itself become much out of use? Has not the whole conformity received a blow? . . . Let them not forecast to preserve it, nor seek to deliver it out of the hand of the Almighty.[44]

Helwys basically stated that God was in the process of judging the Church of England. The evidence of divine judgment was that it was in strong decline. The church did not use the *Common Book* as it once did, nor was the Church practicing its own calendar. The consequences of God's judgment compelled Helwys to admonish "the godly wise that seek salvation" to make a comparison between both beasts with the Scriptures as the standard for ecclesiology.[45]

The Church of England as a Deficient Ecclesiology

Helwys rejected the Church of England as an insufficient ecclesiology on the grounds that the hierarchy has persecuted those who protest against it. The application is that a true church would not resort to violent methods to enforce doctrinal conformity. Since the Anglican Church has a history of brutality, that aspect serves as evidence that God is not a part of something he would condemn. Richard Hooker, who helped establish Anglican Ecclesiology in his work, *Of the Laws of Ecclesiastical Polity: Eight Books*, wrote concerning the king's authority to "prescribe what themselves think good to be done in the service of God, how the word shall be taught, how Sacraments administered; that Kings . . . what causes soever do appertain unto the Courts; that *Kings* and *Queens* in their own proper persons are by judicial sentence to decide the questions which rise about matter of faith and Christian religion."[46]

44. Ibid., 29.

45. Ibid., 30.

46. Hooker, *Of the Laws of Ecclesiastical Polity*, 8:208. Chapter 4 will develop the

The Monarchy often took brutal actions to suppress dissenters. Thus, Helwys argued that the Church of England in its hierarchy had become like Rome. Couple this fact with the pageantry, religious holiday, and the pomp, all serve to remind the membership that it practices Catholicism while attempting to embrace Reformed doctrine. The celebrations of the Church of England move very little toward true reform, which is also evidenced in the titles of the clergy.

The clergy used titles that could only belong to the Lord. By accepting the accolades of those titles, Helwys attributed the nomenclature as being tantamount to blasphemy. This conjured the image of false worship or perhaps even worship of the man of sin. For Helwys, the use of titles could only mean that a human had accepted the honor reserved only for the Lord.

Another problem with the worship of the Church of England was the usage of the *Common Book*. Helwys never claimed it was liturgical, but in essence his denunciation of it was simply because it had replaced the Scriptures. The prayers, the time of the prayers, and the place and hour of those prayers became at best legalistic and at worst irrelevant. The *Common Book* was simply another indication that the heart of worship was lacking, as the ritualism of false worship became the standard. As Helwys bemoaned the *Common Book*, he associated it with priests who were spiritually unqualified and theologically incapable of performing simple pastoral duties.

This unfortunate situation led to a false zealousness that Helwys deemed "false fire."[47] Helwys used this term to say that the clergy of the Church of England "work all their signs and lying wonders," which "stole away" the hearts of men.[48] The false fire was nothing less than satanic activity at work under the guise of ecclesiology. The consequence was that true believers were to reject the Anglican Church as a false church with false fire.

The above scenarios led Helwys to condemn the church as being under the divine judgment of God. The decline in attendance, the decline of the *Common Book*, the inability of the church to produce quality pastors, and the persecution of innocent people are all evidence of this judgement. Helwys regarded the Church of England as nothing less than the second beast that bows to the first beast of Rome.

---

arguments that Helwys uses against the King having divine rights to examine and determine the fate of English citizens.

47. Helwys, *Mystery of Iniquity*, 27.

48. Ibid.

Implications for Baptist Ecclesiology

The fact that Helwys condemned both Roman Catholicism and Anglicanism was indicative that he had determined, or at the very least was developing, a Baptist ecclesiology. In other words, even though his previous works were directed at the Mennonites, they reveal that Helwys based his criticism of the Roman and English churches on the grounds of Baptist ecclesiology. A cursory review of *A Declaration of Faith of the English People Remaining at Amsterdam in Holland*[49] reveals that Helwys had a Baptist ecclesiological foundation as the basis for his criticism of Roman Catholicism and the Church of England.

A Declaration of Faith of the English
People Remaining at Amsterdam

This document has the notoriety of being the very first Baptist confession of faith.[50] The work is a confession of faith that prescribed the theological position of the Helwys faction of the burgeoning Baptist ecclesiology in the year 1611. The significance of the date reveals that Helwys had begun to develop Baptist ecclesiology a year earlier than his work, *A Short Declaration of the Mystery of Iniquity*. Thus, *A Declaration of Faith of the English People Remaining at Amsterdam* established the foundation for the later work.

The *Declaration of Faith* lists twenty-seven articles that are designed to show the differences between the Mennonite church and the faith of the English people at Amsterdam. William Lumpkin writes:

> Obviously it owed much to John Smyth, though it goes beyond his confessions at a number of points: in urging the independence and autonomy of the local church ("though in respect of CHRIST, the Church bee one") in denying a succession in church life, and in rejecting the Mennonite prohibitions against oaths, the bearing of arms, participation in government, and having dealings with excommunicants. It aimed, indeed, to distinguish its authors from the Mennonites.[51]

---

49. Helwys, "Declaration of Faith."

50. Burgess, *John Smith the Se-Baptist*, 212.

51. Helwys, *Declaration of Faith*, 115. The historical setting in which this work was written will be discussed in chapter 5.

Even though the work is directed to the Mennonites, it does reveal the basic ecclesiology that Helwys did not wish to compromise with Rome, England, or the Mennonites.

The ecclesiological foundation that undergirds Helwys's position is found in Article 13, which states:

> That everie Church is to receive in all their members by Baptisme vpon the Confession off their faith and sinness wrought by the preaching off the Gospel, according to the primitive instruction. Matt. 28:19. And practice, Acts 2:41. And therefore Churches constituted after anie other manner, or off anie other persons are not according to CHRISTS Testament.[52]

Helwys does not address the issue of a constituted church with Rome or the Church of England, but he does address it with the Puritans and the Separatists.[53] However, the fact that he directed this Article to the Mennonites serves to provide a basis for Helwys's thought. The churches of Rome and England were not properly constituted. They adhered to pomp and circumstance, religious festivals, and calendars that were not a part of the New Testament design for ecclesiology.

Another article warrants mention as it pertains to Baptist ecclesiology. Helwys indicated that each church was local and visible. He did so by stating the officers of the church were directly related to its own congregation. Article 22 reads

> that the Officers off everie Church of congregation are tied to by Office onely to that particular congregacion whereoff they are chosen, Acts 14:23, and 20:17. Tit. 1:5. And therefore they cannot challenge by office anie aucthoritie in anie other congregation whatsoever except they would have an Apostleship.[54]

That the emphasis on this article is placed upon the officers of the congregation is well-noted. Yet, the officers of a church cannot meet the requirements unless there is a local congregation which they serve. This is tantamount to placing the emphasis of the ministry *at* and *for* the local

---

52. Ibid., 120.

53. Helwys, *Mystery of Iniquity*, 65. Helwys argued that the Puritans had not completed their reform as they remained committed to the Church of England. On page 92, he stated that Separatists voluntarily joining together to form a true church via a covenant are invalid if they retained their infant baptism position. These concepts will be developed in chapter 5.

54. Helwys, "Declaration of Faith," 122.

church body as an Independent church, for example, free from all ecclesiastical control. In effect, Helwys had declared a localism that is now seen by many as part and parcel of Baptist ecclesiology. Thus, in essence, this article serves as foundational for arguments against hierarchical appointments by pope, presbyters, or bishops. Since the local congregation chooses its own minister, that fact alone states that the congregation is the final authority for the local *ecclesia*.

This denounces the position of both pope and English ecclesiastical hierarchy. This simply means that the local congregation has its own authority under the headship of Christ as found in the Scriptures. Helwys states this concept in Article 23.

> That the scriptures off the Old and New Testament are written for our instruction, 2 Tim. 3.16 7 that wee ought to search them for they testifie off CHRIST, Io 5.39. And therefore to bee vsed withal reverence, as conteyning the Holie Word off GOD, which onelie is our direction in al thinges whatsoever.[55]

Additionally, this article means that Helwys's Baptist ecclesiology would not allow a Baptist church to accept the *Common Book*, which had the authority and approval of the Church of England. The Scriptures were at the heart of Helwys's development of Baptist ecclesiology. The Bible, per Helwys's Baptist ecclesiology, would not be placed under the alleged higher rule of a *Common Book*.

The fact is granted that Helwys did not argue the above finer points in Book 1 of *A Short Declaration of the Mystery of Iniquity*. However, the foundation of *Mystery of Iniquity* does reveal an ecclesiology that had been previously developed. Thus, the rationale for his criticism of both Rome and England was not to draw attention to himself, but rather to appeal to the English King on the simple basis that he had discovered ecclesiological truth. The cursory review of *A Declaration of Faith of the English People Remaining at Amsterdam in Holland* displays a rich ecclesiological foundation, which undergirded the arguments of *A Short Declaration of the Mystery of Iniquity*. The earlier confession by Helwys laid the biblical foundation that allows him to address the king in the later treatise on the issue of citizenship, the role of the magisterial church, and the limitation of the English Monarchy.

---

55. Ibid.

4

Helwys's Appeal to the King for Toleration

His Rationale for Rejecting Royal Supremacy

Introduction

IN CHAPTER 2, THE apocalyptic literary connection was made between Helwys's *Mystery of Iniquity* and the works of John Foxe and John Bale. This established the fact that Helwys was following the example of writing about the church in the traditional apocalyptic ecclesiological terms with which England was familiar. In chapter 3, however, instead of supporting the Church of England in their reform attempts, Helwys took the position that the English national church was, like Rome, a false church. He began to condemn the church as a deficient *ecclesia* and also promoted the Baptist church as a biblical alternative. In the present chapter, a review of the English Monarchy will be considered, along with the rise of Royal Supremacy. The chapter will proceed to evaluate Helwys's argument against Royal Supremacy and will conclude with the implications for Baptist ecclesiology.

The Magisterial Reformation changed the direction of Christianity in the sixteenth century by appealing to local governmental support. The rationale for this support was twofold. First, the quest for religious toleration was correctly presumed to be denied by Roman Catholicism. Therefore, a powerful government with an army could insist upon toleration, or the consequences would mean bloodshed. This appeal to local government did little to thwart Roman Catholic aggression and did not procure the desired religious toleration without war. The second reason for the appeal to government is that the covenantal approach to ecclesiology was directly related to the citizenship of the local country; for example, good Lutherans were also good German citizens. The end result is that Magisterial Reformation "did not bring about wholesale demands for religious liberty or separation of church and state."[1] The method for the Magisterial Reformation was to develop and maintain some form of a state-church system.

The English Reformation proceeded with the same magisterial format. The Anglican Church had the theological form of Catholicism, but utilized English nomenclature. Commenting on Henry VIII and the Church of England, Edmund S. Morgan stated, "Since he had few aspirations toward purity, either personal or ecclesiastical, he did his best to keep his popeless church otherwise unchanged and un-Protestant."[2] However, noted scholar Alec Ryrie claims that Henry possessed a misguided sense of purity. He states:

> All of his life, Henry had an enviable power to convince himself that what he wanted to do was in fact the right thing to do. This rendered him almost entirely free of self-doubt, and meant that persuading him to change his mind was formidably difficult. It also made him ready to assume that his opponents were God's enemies. So rather than pursuing mere self-interest, he would deduce general principles from his own interests and apply them more widely, allowing them to take on a life of their own . . . Henry's public justification for pursuing Divorce was that he was stricken in conscience, and utterly convinced that his marriage was an unlawful pretense.[3]

Regardless of personal motive, the end result is that Henry's divorce established the platform for an English national church. William Jordan affirms the English-Catholic-Anglican motif when he stated, "The English Reformation sloughed off the English Church from the Church Universal,

---

1. Yarbrough, "English Separatist Influence," 14.

2. Morgan, *Visible Saints*, 5.

3. Ryrie, *The Age of Reformation*, 113.

though every effort was made by Henry VIII and his divines to retain and maintain the catholic character of the Church."[4]

Henry VIII's efforts produced England with a national church comprised of Englishmen who were loyal to both church and king. The national church replaced the Roman Catholic international or universal church with a membership base that strongly identified with English nationalism.[5] Consequently, the national Church of England was "coterminous with the realm" of English citizens with the English Monarch as the head of both church and state. In order to demonstrate the significance of the Church of England, a brief overview is warranted.

The English Reform Movement

The English Reform was not a religious reform movement in that the desire to transform the Roman Church was pivotal.[6] Rather, the English Reform was motivated by Henry VIII's desire to divorce his wife and seek a different marriage. The English Monarch determined that ecclesiastical matters were under the jurisdiction of the king. Malcolm B. Yarnell III states, "From the central government of England, ecclesiastical dogma was determined and disseminated, even as it was variously received in the life of the local church."[7]

King Henry's Quest for Divorce

The question of Henry VIII's divorce had serious religious ramifications for England. However, Henry W. Clark speculated:

> One is safe in saying that only because that particular object where he was bent happened to be one which brought him into conflict with the pope did religion come into question at all. . . . The fact that the actual change, or "reform," which did take place had to be

---

4. Jordan, *Development of Religious Toleration*, 2:49.

5. Ibid.

6. The review of the English Reform movement will not be exhaustive. Selective highpoints of the movement receive consideration. The rationale for this approach is to demonstrate Helwys's argument for Baptist distinctives within the background of the Church of England and its Head, King James. Therefore, a brief review of the English Reformation is warranted.

7. Yarnell, *Royal Priesthood in the English Reformation*, 123.

> worked in the religious sphere was but an accident of the situation, and no more.[8]

The point Clark makes is rather pointed, albeit truthful. Henry VIII's desire for divorce took on the religious sphere simply because of the divorce and not the need for a reformed church. Thus, the reform in England was not undergirded by religious motives, but rather by personal disposition. Clark goes on to say:

> From one point of view, indeed, the entire movement might almost be called a personal one, inasmuch as it arose from, and tended to, the satisfaction of the King's desires, was in truth a movement affecting the King's personal position first and foremost and other things only incidentally, went to make the King's authority supreme.[9]

The process of Henry VIII's divorce was the catalyst that led to the English Reformation.

The monarch appealed to conscience as his primary avenue for suggesting that marriage to Catherine of Aragon was invalid. Henry came to the conclusion that he truly had violated God's command by marrying Catherine of Aragon. His biblical support was Leviticus 18:26 and 20:21. These verses prohibit marriage to a brother's wife, an act which Henry had committed. Henry took the position that even the pope did not have the right to circumvent the law of God.

The biblical problem Henry encountered was that his circumstance was guided by another principal verse that possessed more significance. The Deuteronomy 25:5 passage commanded that if she was childless, a brother was legally required to marry his brother's widow. In his recent biography entitled *The Tudors*, Richard Rex stated that "this special case exactly described the case of Henry, his brother Arthur, and Catherine of Aragon."[10] This issue was at the forefront of the Monarch's life, and it did impact English society.

A proper assessment of Henry VIII will bring a much-needed balance to the situation of sixteenth-century England. To regard Henry VIII as simply one who wielded power over England for personal gain is to dismiss his reform with prejudice. He did change English society for the

8. Clark, *History of English Nonconformity*, 108.

9. Ibid.

10. Rex, *Tudors*, 60.

better, as his reign is considered the turning point in English History. Rex gives this insight:

> To his reign can be traced the roots of the Church of England, the seeds of the Irish Question, the birth of the English Bible, the founding of the Privy Council, and the principle of the omni-competence of parliamentary statute. His reign saw the destruction of English monasticism, which had helped shape the society and landscape of England for nearly a millennium. As a result, it also witnessed the greatest shift in landholding since the Norman Conquest, and saw the landed wealth of the Crown itself reach its highest level ever. His reign, in short, saw something a little less than a revolution.[11]

No question exists that Henry VIII's contribution to English society propelled the country to the modern world. In fact, his desire for divorce reveals a man who considered commitments somewhat antiquated. Nonetheless, the monarch's contribution to English society laid the foundation for the emergence of modern England.

Politics and Religion

Henry VIII's appeal to the pope for divorce was denied. The uncooperative position of the pope meant that Henry was without biblical precedence as interpreted by Roman Catholicism. From the pope's perspective, the issue of Henry's divorce meant reversing canon law. Henry VIII did not comprehend that the pope had to reverse a decision by a recent predecessor if a divorce was granted. This was not impossible, but it was politically abhorrent to the pope. Henry VIII's request for divorce was simply ill-timed.

The issue, per Roman Catholicism, was complicated to say the least. Catherine of Aragon was the aunt to Charles V, King of Spain. Should the pope have granted Henry's divorce, it would have been tantamount to saying that Catherine of Aragon "had been living in incest for nearly twenty years."[12] The pope wanted to avoid offending Charles V as his army had conquered Northern Italy and surrounded Rome. The pope may have been willing to grant Henry's request. However, Jessica Sharkey stated:

11. Ibid., 46.

12. Ibid., 61.

> These plans were thrown into utter disarray by the news of the
> sack of Rome, which arrived in England at the very beginning of
> June. In a letter to Henry, dated 2 June, the cardinal wrote that the
> sack must stir the hearts of all Christian princes. He warned the
> king that if the pope were to be killed or taken as hostage by the
> emperor it would be to the detriment of Henry's affairs. The cardi-
> nal and the king were both aware of the kinship ties between the
> emperor and Catherine of Aragon, his aunt. While the emperor
> had control over the pope, it was unlikely that the papacy could
> solve the Great Matter in Henry's favour.[13]

The immediate problem confronting the pope was survival of the Spanish
attack, which meant that the pope could not alienate Charles V by supporting Henry VIII.

Another problem that complicated the issue was the Protestant Reformation in general. The pope could not afford to lose another country to
Protestant monarchs. One of the many claims by the Protestants was the
abuse of the papal office. If the pope granted a divorce to Henry VIII, this
would have been more evidence for the Protestants to use against Roman
Catholicism. In other words, the argument of wealth, power, and position, particularly as related to Henry VIII, would be utilized to justify the
Protestant Reform movement. At the same time, the situation was delicate
for the relationship between the pope and Henry VIII. The pope could not
afford to lose the friendship of Henry VIII any more than he could that of
Charles V. However, denial was the safer political decision for the pope.
Therefore, at the risk of offending the English King, Henry VIII's appeal
for divorce was denied.

Royal Supremacy[14]

The pope's denial of Henry VIII's divorce set the English Reformation
in motion. However, the problem was how to convert English Catholic
churches into English Anglican churches? How would the Catholic clergy
become Protestant with their congregations? Who would be head of the
church? If the Church was associated with the English state, where did
ecclesiastical and civil law mutually agree and terminate?

13. Sharkey, "Between King and Pope," 238.

14. The review of Royal Supremacy will not be exhaustive. The foundational arguments will be delineated so as to allow a better understanding of Helwys's concern. For a
thorough analysis of Royal Supremacy, see Yarnell, *Royal Priesthood*.

The answers to these questions were indirectly addressed and answered by the Catholic Pope. The divorce trial Henry VIII requested took place in the ecclesiastical court in London. Catherine of Aragon appealed to the pope to have the trial moved from London to Rome, citing that she would not receive a fair trial. The pope acquiesced and consequently, but not unexpectedly, Henry VIII was furious and thus determined to lead England out of Roman Catholicism. Ryrie confirms that Henry was convinced he was appointed by God to lead the political and religious life of England.

> By the time it was achieved, the Royal Supremacy over the Church was more than simply a means to the Divorce. Rather, the long struggle with Rome over the Divorce had convinced Henry that Rome's authority was false. We do not know when, how or through whom Henry VIII arrived at his developed doctrine of Royal Supremacy. But whether or not it was he who had the idea, by the early 1530s it is clear that the idea had him. It became one of his core convictions that God had appointed him as the Supreme Head of the English Church.[15]

In other words, Henry VIII was king by divine rights. Thus, when Wolsey failed to secure Henry's divorce, he was disposed to his diocese of York as a punishment for failing the divinely appointed King of England. Soon, when "summoned to London in 1530 to face charges of treason, Wolsey was lucky enough to die en route, thus cheating the headsman."[16]

Again, to dismiss Wolsey from the establishment of Royal Supremacy is deficient in understanding his contributions to the establishment of the Anglican Church.

> Wolsey himself played a part in the development of the royal supremacy. As chancellor, the keeper of the court of the king's conscience, he attempted and largely succeeded in dominating common law, and as papal legate *a latere*, Wolsey ruled the English church. This monopolizing combination of the jurisdictions of church and state meant that, "In fact, though not in form, he was the first who wielded sovereignty in England because he ruled both church and state."[17]

15. Ryrie, *Age of Reformation*, 128.

16. Rex, *Tudors*, 63.

17. Pollard, *Wolsey*, 372, quoted in Yarnell, *Royal Priesthood*, 127.

The combination of ecclesiastical law with civil law was the legacy of Wolsey. The direction of the English Church under the authority of the English Monarch still exists today.

Anticlericalism

The problem was that the clerics favored Catherine of Aragon and the decision of the pope. As long as the clerics were loyal to Rome and Catherine, Henry VIII was limited to their ecclesiastical jurisdiction. However, Henry, acting as the Vicar of Christ in the English realm, began to fine the clergy for violating "the ancient statute of *praemunire* through being accomplices, so to speak, in Wolsey's exercise of his powers as papal legate in England . . . The Defender of the Faith was beginning to attack the Church."[18] The use of the ancient law of *praemunire*[19] was designed to bring the clerics into agreement with the king. In his article, "Henry VIII and the Praemunire Manoeuvres of 1530–1531," J. A. Guy stated:

> Henry VIII wanted the province to purchase quickly an expensive pardon for "illegal" exercising of spiritual jurisdiction, and to acknowledge him forthwith as "sole protector and supreme head of the English church and clergy"—whatever that meant in 1531. Terms of a compromise were hammered out, and it might be thought that the *manoeuvres* were concluded when the king accepted a clerical subsidy of £100,000 and the title of supreme head "as far as Christ's law allows."[20]

The purpose of this was to ensure the support of the English clergy. The clergy had no choice but to recognize Henry VIII, the English Monarch who held the power of the authority of Rome in matters of the English Church.

The clergy was accustomed to an independent mindset that was not dictated by the king. Russell Conrad states that "from 1534 to 1640 the clergy's claim to an independent jurisdiction, as well as their independent

---

18. Rex, *Tudors*, 63.

19. Cross and Livingston, *Oxford Dictionary of the Christian Church*, s.v. "Praemunire." This law "was designed to protect rights claimed by the English Crown against encroachment by the Papacy . . . The statute of 1353 forbade the withdrawal from England of cases which should be decided in the king's court, and the penalties prescribed were in 1393 stiffened and extended to any who should promote any papal bull translating to others sees bishops on whom the king depended as ministers of state. . . ."

20. Guy, "Henry VIII and the *Praemunire Manoeuvres* of 1530–1531," 481.

legislative power, were matters of recurring dispute."[21] In short, the clergy was being forced to embrace Protestantism in the name of English nationalism. Torrance Kirby stated:

> Clearly recognizing the anti-papal writing on the wall, the clergy in Convocation initiated a pre-emptive attempt at a systematic overhaul of the canon law four years before the break with Rome was formally sealed. The canon law together with its complex apparatus of courts, procedures, and precedents was so closely bound up with papal authority that the flexing of royal claims to supreme ecclesiastical jurisdiction provided an irresistible impetus to constitutional and legal reform.[22]

The end result of this Convocation was the infamous Act of Submission, in May 1532, which recognized the rule of Henry VIII as head of the Church.

The clergy offered the Act of Submission to royal evaluation by Parliament. The Act of Submission references the thirty-two member committee that essentially reformed canon law. As Kirby demonstrated, the reform of the canon law was twenty years before concrete action could be taken, but it did result in the establishment of the king as head of the Church of England.

> So that finally whichsoever of the said constitutions, ordinance or canons provincial of synodal shall be thought and determined by your grace, and by the most part of the said thirty-two persons, not to stand with God's laws, and the laws of the realm, the same to be abrogated and taken away by your grace, and the clergy. And such of them as shall be seen by your grace, and by the most part of the said thirty-two persons stand with God's laws, and the laws of your realm, to stand in full strength and power, your grace's most royal assent and authority once obtained fully given to the same.[23]

The consequences of this action allowed Henry VIII to name Thomas Cranmer Archbishop of Canterbury, in order to achieve his divorce from Catherine Aragon and to marry Anne Boleyn.

---

21. Conrad, "Parliament, the Royal Supremacy and the Church," 27.

22. Kirby, "Lay Supremacy," 352.

23. Ibid., 353. Kirby is quoting Wilkens, *Concilia Magnae Britanniae et Heberniae*, 3:754–55; and Gee and Hardy, *Documents Illustrative of English Church History*, 176–78.

Act of Supremacy 1534

"The Supremacy of the Crown Act 1534 confirms to Henry VIII and his successors the title of 'The only Supreme Head in Earth of the Church of England, called *Anglicana Ecclesia*.'"[24] This action recognized the ecclesiastical authority of the King of England and his successors. Per Rex, "The act was carefully phrased to make it clear that Parliament was recognizing the king's supremacy in the Church, and not conferring it upon him."[25] This act meant that the local congregant and congregation possessed no authority to determine their own ministries under the headship of Christ.

The problem with the Act of Supremacy is that any form of religious toleration could be interpreted to mean heresy, which then became a political crime. Jordan addressed this issue:

> When the State assumes the task of directing the Church, heresy will inevitably become a political crime, or at least an offense which will be judged by political concerns. The theological formulae will still be employed but the application will become increasingly devoid of spiritual content. . . . Men will soon question the competence of the civil power to determine religious truths; for the judgment of what is and what is not heresy involves capability.[26]

The issue of a Church-State relationship means that the political sphere controls the religious realm. Thus, all internal religious issues are politicized by the unfortunate church-state union and are decided upon by the politician and not the congregation, following the guidance of the Holy Spirit. The Act of Supremacy now ensured the King as the arbiter of heresy and loyalty to the English Crown.

One other issue is noteworthy as it relates to the Act of Supremacy. Most English citizens now found themselves converted to Anglicanism. This was not a willful conversion, but rather one forced upon them. The adage was that English citizens were now English churchmen. No option existed for them to embrace unless of course they wanted to face charges of treason. Even though A. H. Newman is writing of the Protestant Reformation in Lutheranism, his insight into forced or compulsory church

---

24. Cross and Livingston, *Oxford Dictionary of the Christian Church*, s.v. "Supremacy."

25. Rex, *Tudors*, 80.

26. Jordan, *Development of Religious Toleration*, 2:69.

membership is valid for England. He depicted this situation as one that was flawed with innate problems. Newman stated:

> First, the political relations of states are such that they rarely move without reference to temporal interest. . . . Secondly, admitting, as a possibility, the purely religious motives of the authorities in any politico-religious movement, the consciences of the people and their religious ideas are not the consciences and ideas of the authorities. The people, as a body, were at that time, very likely to conform outwardly to the ecclesiastical arrangements of their rulers; yet who would be credulous enough to think that the entire spiritual status of a whole nation could be changed in a day or in a year? The Spirit of God does not work that way. Thirdly, the very process of transferring people suddenly from one communion to another, without any exercise of volition on their part, tends to foster in their minds the notion that religion is a mere matter of form.[27]

Newman was accurate about forced or compulsory church membership. England continued to refine its Anglicanism for the next seventy-five years.

Newman's critique of the state-church union is accurate, as the Act of Supremacy reveals the extent of political-religious power in England. The Preamble to the Act of Supremacy stated:

> And that our said sovereign lord, his heirs and successors kings of this realm, shall have full power and authority from time to time to visit, repress, redress, reform, order, correct, restrain and amend all such errors, heresies, abuses, offences, contempts, and enormities, whatsoever they be, which by an manner spiritual authority or jurisdiction ought or may lawfully be reformed, repressed, ordered, redressed corrected, restrained or amended, most to the pleasure of Almighty God, the increase of virtue in Christ's religion, and for the conservation of the peace, unity and tranquility of this realm: any usage, custom, foreign laws, foreign authority, prescription of any other thing or things to the contrary hereof notwithstanding.[28]

The Crown was granted religious power over the country, which included the responsibility of keeping heresy and heretics at bay. The English Reform was now moving toward Anglicanism. The next step was to solidify the continuation of reform for the next generation.

27. Newman, "Reformation from a Baptist Point of View," 9.

28. Elton, *Tudor Constitution*, 364–65.

King Edward VI

Even though Henry VIII had an affinity for Catholicism, he made certain that his son was well-trained in Protestantism. John Cheke held Protestant evangelical views and "was chosen because he was the brightest star in a constellation of talent emerging at Cambridge University and, above all, was associated with Saint Johns' College—a college of academic excellence, which was rapidly becoming a bridgehead of the English Reformation."[29]

Edward was only nine years old when he assumed the English Throne as king.[30] Edward's coronation, in February 1547, was supervised by Thomas Cranmer and other notable Protestants such as Hugh Latimer. The charge to young Edward was to "emulate the Old Testament King Josiah."[31] The Duke of Somerset, Edward's uncle, wasted no time in moving the nation more to the Protestant position as injunctions were issued on July 31, 1547. These injunctions were designed to eliminate Catholic mass.[32] English religion was transformed within two years.

Act of Uniformity 1549

During the winter of 1548–49, Cranmer seized the opportunity to write an English form of worship entitled the *Book of Common Prayer (BCP)*.[33] The work was enforced by the Act of Uniformity going into effect on Whit Sunday, June 9, 1549.[34] The Act of Uniformity was designed to impose "exclusive use of the *First Book of Common Prayer . . .* from the ensuing Whit Sunday in the celebration of the Lord's Supper, commonly called the Mass and in all public services."[35] This legal act ended the Latin Mass, which was

---

29. Rex, *Tudors*, 144–45.

30. Henry had established an advisory committee, known as the Privy Council, which was directed by Edward Seymour, the uncle of Edward VI.

31. Rex, *Tudors*, 151.

32. Per Rex, the parishioners were to remove private and public devotional images, and no longer recite the rosary. Parish priests were to admonish the congregants not to leave money for Mass (and for their souls), funds for the parish were to be diverted to the poor, all candles were to be extinguished, holy water was forbidden, and no procession were allowed on Sundays and feast days. See *Tudors*, 153.

33. See chapter 3 for purpose of the *Book of Common Prayer*.

34. Rex, *Tudors*, 156.

35. Cross and Livingston, *Oxford Dictionary of the Christian Church*, s.v. "Uniformity, Acts of."

the only style of worship England had ever known since the written history of the country. This was done so that the English Reform movement would assert an "entirely new English service with a very different underlying theology . . . Nothing like it had ever been envisaged, let alone attempted, in the entire history of Christianity."[36]

The Protestant Reformation on the Continent was started with religious reformers, not German nobility or politicians. Thus, a unified worship in the region was not even remotely a consideration. However, the Act of Uniformity was nothing less than governmental insistence that Anglican Worship make a decisive break with Roman Catholic Latin Mass by replacing it with a thorough English approach on the same day. Rex commented:

> Thanks to print, it was possible for a brand new religious service to be celebrated in the 8,000 or so churches of England on one and the same Sunday in accordance with a government decree for which there was little, if any, popular support. The mere success of this measure is a tribute to the capacity of the Tudor administration.[37]

The Act of Uniformity ensured the transition from English Catholicism to English Anglicanism on a single day of worship.

The Forty-Two Articles

The problem of canonical orders had to be addressed. What was the doctrinal practice of the Church of England? Cranmer revised the *BCP* that was more radical than the previous version concerning Anglican worship practice. The 1549 *Book of Common Prayer* was still entrenched in a medieval approach to worship, which meant that Catholic undertones were present. Quoting Diarmaid MacCulloch, Yarnell comments, "The continuities between medieval forms and the 1549 BCP were only a 'stopgap' measure to further reformation in the 1552 *BCP*, and if the Protestant regime had survived, perhaps beyond."[38] Cranmer's desire was a sweeping reform that would bring lasting change to England's worship practice.

The revised *BCP* was delineated in the subsequent Forty-Two Articles that expounded upon the official teachings of the Church of England. Kirby has a lengthy, but significant comment:

36. Rex, *Tudors*, 156.
37. Ibid., 157.
38. Yarnell, *Royal Priesthood*, 200–201.

> These Forty-Two Articles were published shortly before Edward's death on 6 July following. When the Forty-Two Articles were issued under royal authority in 1553 they constituted arguably the most thorough and advanced systematic expression of Reformed doctrine at that time. In doctrinal substance, particularly on crucial matters concerning Grace and the Sacraments, the Articles are comparable to both the French Confession of 1559 and the Second Helvetic Confession of 1566, authored by Jean Calvin and Heinrich Bullinger respectively. On matters of ecclesiastical polity and discipline the Articles lean more towards Zurich than Geneva.[39]

Cranmer was rapidly moving the English Church to a reformed position, and at the same time destroying the Catholic foundations of the church.

Edward died very young halting the reform movement; however, if not for his death, Rex speculates that "Catholicism in England would have disappeared as totally as it did in Zürich and Geneva."[40] Edward's premature death allowed the notorious queen to attempt to return the nation to Catholicism.

Queen Mary

Mary was the illegitimate daughter of Henry VIII. Her birth was not out-of-wedlock, but the divorce of Henry from Mary's mother, Catherine of Aragon, held repercussions for Mary's legal status. The divorce was more of an annulment than a legal divorce, which meant that Mary was deemed illegitimate. Consequently, in 1534, she was denied the ability to be in succession for the throne. In 1544, it was restored without the revocation of her illegitimacy. Regardless of this fact, she thwarted a coup and became the first regnant Queen of England.

Like her mother, Mary was deeply committed to the Catholic faith. After her coronation in the summer of 1553, her primary agenda was to restore Roman Catholicism to England. By Christmas, 1553, the *Book of Common Prayer* was made illegal. She released Roman Catholic priests from prison and imprisoned Anglican bishops such as Thomas Cranmer. Harrison Crumrine states:

> Consequently, the regime began to target reform leaders in order to make an example of them as well as to silence the opposition. On

---

39. Kirby, "Articles of Religion of the Church of England."

40. Rex, *Tudors*, 166.

20 July 1553, Marian authorities imprisoned Bishop Nicholas Ridley in the Tower of London. Bishop Hugh Latimer joined him on 4 September, and Archbishop Thomas Cranmer followed on 13 September. These reform leaders went to the stake in 1555 at Oxford.[41]

The first two years of Mary's reign saw the developed movement of a Catholic restoration to England. Rex affirms this conclusion:

> From the start of her reign, Mary was determined to restore the old religion in its fullness, and before she even arrived in London she had sent letters to Pope Julius III with a view to reconciling England with Rome . . . Mary had steadfastly held to the Mass under Edward, so it was no surprise when she promptly set about dismantling the Edwardine Reformation.[42]

Mary was determined to return England to Roman Catholicism regardless of her father or half-brother's advancements toward Protestantism.

Cardinal Pole was chosen to negotiate reconciliation with Roman Catholicism. Even though he was a cousin to Henry VIII, he argued against the king's divorce. Along with the issue that he was favored by the pope, this fact was appealing to Mary. Pole had successfully convinced Parliament that reconciliation with Rome was much more desirable for a unified country. By November 1554, Parliament had voted to reconcile with Rome, and the country was subsequently granted absolution.[43]

The Burning of Protestants

At first, the reaction to Protestantism was an ultimatum to leave the country. The option to revert back to Catholicism was possible, though not probable for those who were committed to the English Reformation. Champlin Burrage reported:

> In this predicament the Reformation leaders of the Church of England and the people who sympathized with them, we are told, were themselves, "separated from the rest of the Lande, as from the world, and ioyned in couenaunt, by voluntarie profession [evidently much as were the Scottish Reformers in time of special danger], to obey the trueth of Christ, and to witness against the

41. Crumrine, "Oxford Martyrs and the English Protestant Movement," 75.

42. Rex, *Tudors*, 190.

43. Ibid., 192.

abominations of Antichrist, As they also did euen vnto death, in the trueth which they sawe, though otherwise being but as it were in the twilight of the Gospell they had their wantes and errors." It is said that during Mary's reign several hundred people fled from the country.[44]

The act of the many Reformers who fled England has become known as the Marian Exile.[45]

The Exiles are estimated to number nearly eight hundred. According to Barbara Griswold, "at least 800 Protestants went into exile in Germany and Switzerland."[46] However, many of the Protestants could not leave England. The misfortune of these Protestants reveals one of the saddest periods in the history of England.

The old English law passed in 1401, *De Heretica Comburendo* (on the burning of heretics) was used by Mary to force conformity to English Catholicism. Even though this law was repealed in 1547, it was restored and placed in effect in January 1555.[47] This meant that those who could not leave the land would lose their lives for their Protestant religion. Benjamin Evans states, "In 1554, Pole ordered a visitation to be held throughout the whole country. A book was to be kept, in which the names of conformists were to be entered, and the separatists were to be reported, and proceeded against with the utmost severity of the law."[48]

Apparently, Queen Mary or Cardinal Pole decided to prepare for the enforcement of the renewed ancient law. The law was designed to burn the dissenter who was deemed heretical. When the era was complete, nearly three hundred people had been burned at the stake in the name of heresy.[49]

44. Francis Johnson's statement, published in Jacob, *Defense of the Churches and Ministry of Englande*, 13, quoted in Burrage, *Early English Dissenters*, 70.

45. Firth, *Apocalyptic Tradition*; see chapter 3 for a review of the Marian Exiles in Europe.

46. Griswold, "Congregational Dynamics," 13.

47. Rex, *Tudors*, 196.

48. Evans, *Early English Baptists*.

49. Ibid. Evans has a lengthy quote, but one worthy of mention. "For no crime did these men suffer. Against them no charge of rebellion, conspiracy, or disloyalty, was ever urged. Their secret meetings had no hostile design against their cruel oppressors. They stand before us untainted by any civil crimes. Their bitterest foes are silent on these matters. They are 'fanatics,' detested, the enemies of the church; their principles are subversive of all ecclesiastical rule, and the fruits of Satanic influence; their destruction would be a blessing to the church and the nation,—phrases like these, and opinions kindred to them, may be found in abundance; but even Bonner and his harpies never allege other

The reign of Mary is well-known for the martyrdoms of the English Protestants. B. R. White makes an interesting observation concerning the martyrs. He stated, "The notably high proportion of artisan Protestant martyrs under Mary is a standing testimony to the effective advancement of Protestant convictions among the people at large under Edward."[50] Mary had failed to restore Catholicism, but she did save it. The Catholic Church exists in England today as a legacy of her determined, albeit brutal reign.

Queen Elizabeth

Mary died without child and, thus, without an heir to the throne. No other choice presented but to recognize her half-sister Elizabeth as the rightful heir to the English throne. Elizabeth was the daughter of Anne Boleyn and, as such, she had Protestant tendencies, but she held these convictions seemingly out of a sense of personal survival—not necessarily a religious conviction. Rex stated:

> It was the circumstances of her birth, rather than any sentimental attachment to her mother's memory, that determined Elizabeth's religious stance. As the papacy had never recognized Henry's divorce as valid, while the King claimed that his marriage to Catherine of Aragon was against scripture itself, it was on the authority of the Bible alone, of the Bible as opposed to the Catholic Church, that Elizabeth based her very right to the throne, and in a sense her very right to life.[51]

---

charges. They were disloyal to Rome, but not to England's queen. They claimed the right to think and judge for themselves on the great matters of the present and the future life. From this circle they excluded all influence. Monarchs, popes, councils, bishops, were not allowed to speak. Only One voice was heard, only One authority was recognized. To catch the voice of Jesus, to bow implicitly and reverently to his authority, was the great business of their life. Boldly they avowed this. Collision with Rome was inevitable. With the spiritual despot they grappled. Against his usurped power they swore eternal hostility, and by their teaching and patience in death they inoculated the *public mind with* the only true principles of civil and spiritual freedom. To this comparatively small and hidden spring we must trace back the deep and expanding stream of freedom which we now enjoy."

50. White, *English Separatist Tradition*, 3–4.

51. Rex, *Tudors*, 218.

Elizabeth simply did not have any personal feeling for the Catholic Church. She was the first child to have lived in the Protestant world of both mother and father. Catholicism was not a part of her life.

The practical aspect of rejecting Catholicism was her own disposition. Per the Roman Catholic Church, she could never be anything other than an illegitimate person. If she were to try and obtain papal dispensation, that would have the effect of legitimizing her status and also accepting some form of papal authority over her reign. This was unthinkable. The politically expedient move would be to embrace Protestantism. However, she was not a confirmed Protestant. She "indulged in relatively risk-free gestures which indicated her real sympathies."[52] However, Ryrie, counter to Rex, does state that Elizabeth was more of a convicted Protestant than often realized.

> She was, apparently, a conviction Protestants of sorts. Like her father, she was unswerving in asserting her own authority over the English Church, although she never wielded that authority with his recklessness. She had no patience with what she saw as superstition; she welcomed the translation of the Bible and liturgy into English; and (we can put it no more strongly than this) she seems to have accepted most of the central doctrines of Reformed Protestantism.[53]

Elizabeth was a Protestant, and she supported the Protestant church of her father.

From the English political view, the realm of subjects was faced with three different political Monarchs in less than a decade. The Edwardian Monarchy was decidedly Protestant, but with the coming of Mary, the pendulum had swung the official religion back to Catholicism. With the Elizabethan advent, the official religion was expected to be Protestant. Yet, many English Catholics were loyal subjects. The forces of politics and the constant changing of each new monarch with his/her specific preference for official religion had brought the country to disunity. Elizabeth truly had inherited a divided country.

---

52. Ibid., 219.

53. Ryrie, *Age of Reformation*, 195.

The Middle-Way.

Elizabeth wanted to unite the English empire, and the common thought of the day was that a united empire must have a united religion. Christopher Hill commented, "It was the duty of kings to reduce subjects to obedience to Christ, and they had a special duty to reform clergy."[54] The queen was no advocate for either Protestantism or Catholicism, but only wanted peace and order to her realm; however, "she would not permit the exercise of fanatical zeal."[55]

During the year 1559, two significant actions began to shape the Elizabethan reign: first, the reestablishment of royal supremacy and, second, the reenactment of the *Book of Common Prayer*. The BCP was amended, "which made a few concessions to Catholics."[56] The Act of Supremacy received wide support. "The Act was an assertion of the Monarch's responsibility before God for the welfare of the Church, and annexed 'forever' the power of reforming abuses to the Crown."[57] However, The Act of Uniformity "passed by only three votes."[58] Elizabeth did attempt to bring a settlement to the issue of religion. Griswold stated:

> one must understand the nature of the church she inherited, and was trying to preserve against a resurgence of papal power from within the realm. She tried to resurrect a Protestantism that her predecessor had outlawed by abolishing mass and replacing it with the Lord's Supper in two kinds, adapting the Edwardian Second Prayer Book, removing images, and reducing the 42 Articles to 39, with as little aggravation as possible of her Roman Catholic subjects, with the aid of the 1558 and 1559 Westminster Conferences.[59]

The Elizabethan Settlement was a compromise that did not work well. She did not embrace a thorough reform, nor did she abolish Catholicism. Rex commented, "It is unlikely that anybody apart from the queen herself

---

54. Hill, *Antichrist*, 13.

55. Jordan, *Development of Religious Toleration*, 2:85.

56. Cross and Livingston, *Oxford Dictionary of the Christian Church*, s.v. "Elizabeth I."

57. Ibid., s.v. "Supremacy, Acts of."

58. Rex, *Tudors*, 224.

59. Griswold, "Congregational Dynamics," 25.

envisaged what was done as a 'settlement' with all the finality implied by the term."[60]

Queen Elizabeth continued her approach to the Middle-Way, but it was not without consequences. Her lack of actions gave rise to Puritanism and eventually to Separatism.[61] However, Royal Supremacy would not allow toleration for those sects that wanted reform, much less Independent congregations. Yarnell articulates that part of the reason for the lack of toleration was "when advanced Protestants thought they could compel doctrinal changes, she reminded them she was anointed their queen and no changes could be forced upon her."[62]

King James I

Queen Elizabeth suppressed the Reform movement by allowing moderate toleration, but not conceding to thorough reform per the Puritan agenda. Upon her death in 1603, the Stuart Monarchy era began, which brought with it a renewed sense of possibilities for the Puritans and the Separatists. The new king of England was James VI of Scotland who "was coming from a region that had championed the Reformed cause during the Reformation and enjoyed an established Reformed church."[63]

The sense of Puritan revival was so strong that an ill-advised Millenary Petition was sent to the future king while en route to London. Culpepper described the contents of the document:

> The name was derived from the assertion of its bearers that it was endorsed by a thousand ministers, though only 800 had signed the actual document . . . The petition addressed the form of worship with a specific focus on the wearing of the surplice, the necessity of ensuring that worthy persons entered the ministry of the Church of England, reforms of church livings and maintenance with special concern directed at pluralism, and the matter of church discipline with an insistence that excommunication be levied only with care.[64]

60. Rex, *Tudors*, 224. Rex acknowledges the term as a twentieth-century phrase describing the sixteenth-century event.

61. Puritanism and Separatism will be reviewed in chapters 5 and 6.

62. Yarnell, *Royal Priesthood*, 262.

63. Culpepper, *Francis Johnson and the English Separatist Influence*, 168.

64. Ibid., 168–69.

James VI understood the wider implications of the petition; for instance, if he capitulated to the desires of the petition, the Puritans would elicit other demands. Therefore, the renewed sense of Puritan reform was deemed to be misguided.

The Puritans never considered the possibility that James VI was also a strong monarch with an affinity toward royal supremacy. Michael A. G. Haykin gives insight into this issue as he writes:

> They wrongly assumed that a man with such a pedigree would be amenable to their theological and liturgical concerns, which were quite similar to those of their Scottish brethren. They were wrong. James was imbued with a deeply-rooted conviction of the divine right of kings, namely, that the monarch derives his political legitimacy from God alone and therefore cannot be held accountable by any earthly authority.[65]

The king was disinterested in advancing the Puritan reform. However, he did not disregard the Puritans' demand in totality. King James decided to convene an ecclesiastical conference in order to resolve the issues of the Millenary Petition.

Hampton Court Conference

The conference was an attempt to appease the Puritans and work with the Anglicans to form a peaceful settlement for the Church of England. The Puritans desired a thorough reform toward Calvinism and away from the Catholic vestiges of the church.

The Puritans did not want to separate from the church, but rather to reform it or purify it by means of reform. However, King James wanted conformity to the Church of England with the recognition that he was its head. J. Stephen Phillips comments on the attitude and approach of James I:

> James rejected out of hand the Puritan requests for church reform . . . James made his position clear, "no bishop, no king." According to William Barlow's report, James said of the Puritans that "I will make them conform themselves, or else I will harry them out of the land, or else do worse . . . With his new archbishop, Richard Bancroft, James approved 104 new, rigorous canons to which all clergy must agree or suffer deprivation.[66]

65. Haykin, "Zeal to Promote the Common Good," 21.

66. Phillips, "Thomas Helwys and the Idea of Religious Liberty," 140–41.

The King did not allow any form of religious toleration within England. In fact, the aftermath of the Hampton Court Conference saw the ranks of Separatism swell regardless of the fact that they "became lightning rods for the wrath of the king and his prelates."[67]

Summary of the English Reform Movement

The English Reform movement assumed the same position as the Magisterial Reformers in that the church and state were controlled under the magistrate. Under the leadership of the monarchy, the Church of England became the persecuting church of dissidents. By doing so, the church ultimately served the purpose of the earthly king. Any proposal for reform, much less for religious toleration, was viewed as diametrically opposed to church (the dissident was deemed heretical) and state (the charge of treason was levied against the dissident). Yet the desire for English toleration did not remain silent as the cry for conscience thundered across the English Channel. It was heard from Thomas Helwys, a fledgling General Baptist Church pastor in Amsterdam.

Baptist Ecclesiology and Separation
of Church and State

Within a few years of the Hampton Court Conference, Thomas Helwys addressed King James in Book II of *The Mystery of Iniquity*. Helwys stayed with his motif of apocalyptic literature as he states that "kings cannot serve the Lamb and the beast, but they must needs hate the one and love the other."[68] He argued that the King is appointed by God "to give our Lord the king power to demand and take what he wills of his subjects, and it is to be yielded to him, and to command what ordinance of man he will, and we are to obey it."[69]

Even though he used the apocalyptic motif, Helwys does not call for the destruction of the king, but rather acknowledged that the king has the right to rule his earthly subjects. In fact, Helwys states that "we meddle not with any conditions of contracts made between the king and his

---

67. Griswold, "Congregational Dynamics," 234.

68. Helwys, *Mystery of Iniquity*, 32.

69. Ibid., 33.

people. . . ."[70] The argument concerns the physical realm of the kingdom or England, and Helwys states that all Englishmen are bound to obey the king's laws as they are connected to the welfare of England.

The issue Helwys addressed concerns the spiritual kingdom of God. Utilizing John 18:36–37 and John 17:14, Helwys demonstrated that Christians belong to a spiritual kingdom that is not of this world, nor are the subjects of his kingdom of this world.[71] The spiritual kingdom is not ruled by an earthly king but by Christ who is King alone. Helwys argues:

> And yet this King was in the world and His subjects are in the world (verse 12); and that with this kingdom our lord the king has nothing to do (by his kingly power) but as a subject himself; and that Christ is King alone, only high priest and chief bishop; and there is no king, no primate, metropolitan, archbishop, lord spiritual, but Christ only, nor may be, either in name or power to exercise authority one over another.[72]

The point Helwys makes is that the king has no jurisdiction over the spiritual kingdom of Christ. Helwys goes on to say, "Far be it from the heart of our lord the king to give his earthly power to any to rule as lords over the kingdom and heritage of Christ, which he has reserved to himself to rule and govern only by his Word and Spirit, where no earthly power may be admitted in that it is no earthly kingdom."[73]

The dividing line for Helwys was the earthly realm of God's work through the king and the spiritual realm of Christ's work in the lives of Christians. Helwys did not see the two as incompatible, but rather as complementary. Helwys states:

> Then let our lord the king in all happiness and prosperity sit in his own princely throne of that mighty kingdom of Great Britain, which God has given to the king and to his posterity. And the Lord give the king a most wise heart to rule and judge his people. And the Lord give all his people faithful hearts to love and obey him. And let all those the king's enemies that would not that he should reign over them be slain before him.[74]

70. Ibid.
71. Ibid., 34.
72. Ibid.
73. Ibid.
74. Ibid., 39.

The issue for Helwys was that the two kingdoms (earthly and spiritual) can be inhabited by the Christian without the need for disloyalty to either kingdom.[75] Thus, Helwys's contribution to Baptist ecclesiology is found in the area of which a Christian can be subject to both kingdoms as long as both kingdoms are mutually separate.

The Sword and the Word

The first issue Helwys tackled was the proper use of civil punishment. He acknowledged the position of the king and civil servants as having the authority to use capital punishment for those who are civilly disobedient to the king. "For an earthly sword is ordained of God only for an earthly power, and a spiritual sword for a spiritual power, And offenses against the earthly power must be punished with the earthly sword, and offenses against the spiritual power with a spiritual sword."[76] While recognizing the power of civil authorities, Helwys also acknowledged that rebellion against spiritual powers was to be dealt with by a spiritual sword. This meant that the king and civil authorities had no jurisdiction over spiritual matters.

In order to prove his point, Helwys used Queen Mary as a pertinent illustration. As recalled, Mary used force to compel the people to become Roman Catholic. Even though the sword was used, it had little effect in accomplishing the main goal of making English Christians conform to Roman Catholicism.

The above illustration led Helwys to affirm that spiritual hierarchies did not possess the biblical warrant to use force against those who spiritually rebelled against them. Their power is derived from the King of England. It is an illegitimate power in the sense that only one king is present in the spiritual realm. Thus, Helwys appealed to the king for him to recognize that he is a citizen of the spiritual kingdom and as such could not be a ruler in the same spiritual kingdom. "The King must needs grant that as he is an earthly king he can have no power to rule in this spiritual kingdom of Christ, nor can compel any to be subjects thereof, as a king, while the king is but a subject himself."[77]

Helwys continued to press his point with the illustration of Jesus Christ. The sword is not to be used in matters of religion. Luke 9:52, 56

---

75. Luther made this argument in his 1523 sermon entitled, "Temporal Authority."

76. Helwys, *Mystery of Iniquity*, 35.

77. Ibid., 39.

set the theological platform for Helwys to denounce the use of the sword for matters of religious conversion. The passage reveals that sinful nature of the apostles as they wanted the Lord to call fire down from heaven and consume unrepentant Samaritans. Helwys commented that the king must understand the example of Jesus being non-violent. Helwys wrote:

> Whereby the king does see that Christ will have no man's life touched for his cause. If the Samaritans will not receive him, he passes them by. If the Gadarenes pray him to depart, he leaves them. If any refuse to receive his disciples, he only bids them "shake off the dust of their feet for a witness against them." Here is no sword of justice at all required or permitted to smite any for refusing Christ.[78]

King Christ never resorted to the use of force to compel worship. No biblical example existed to which the king could appeal in order to justify the physical use of the sword for spiritual matters.

Helwys continued on to say that the lesser use of capital punishment, such as banishment, imprisonments, and persecutions, were not the instruments that Christ utilized to force religious conformity. Helwys addressed the issue when he wrote:

> All these instructions and directions are for our lord the king, to direct the king how he should go in and out with holiness and all meekness before his people to win them to Christ, and not to set up a cruel hierarchy to make havoc of the king's people (as Saul did), pulling them out of their homes, both men and women, casting them into prisons, forcing them to flee the land, and persecuting them with all cruelty . . . The king's servants show the king yet once again in all humility that Christ the King did not so himself? He never appointed to be punished any one man for disobeying his gospel, with the least bodily punishment.[79]

Helwys thoroughly denounced the use of the sword as a means to force religious conformity. In fact, he even asked the king to "take his sword out of these lord bishops' hands."[80] This leaves open the issue as to which instrument was at the disposal of both bishop and heretic. Helwys's answer was the Word.

78. Ibid., 38.
79. Ibid., 58–59.
80. Ibid., 49.

Helwys did not leave the issue of religious dissent without a means of settling disputes. He appealed to the king to allow the Scriptures to settle ecclesiological issues. Helwys wrote:

> But all this is to be done only by the King of Israel's power, who has all power given him in heaven and earth, whose power is all-sufficient to bring under obedience all his subjects whereunto no earthly power can be helpful, whose sword is his Word, "which is lively and mighty in operation and sharper than any two-edged sword (Hebrews 4:12) and therefore needs not the help of any king's sword.[81]

The appeal to the Scriptures for ecclesiological issues was supported by the apocalyptic interpretation that King Henry VIII freed the English people from the first beast.

Brian Haymes gives insight into Helwys's rationale for citing the historic event of King Henry VIII:

> Citing what he takes to be a good example of King Henry VIII, who freed the people from the bondage to the first Beast, Helwys hoped James will do the same with the excesses of this rising second Beast who keep the people in cruel bondage which insists that only the bishops have the true interpretation of the Word and that they determine how God is to be worshipped with appointed prayers.[82]

The reference to Henry VIII is made simply because Helwys understood the Church of England to be the second beast exercising the power of the first beast. The referent nuanced the inability of the English people to interpret the Word so that they were without the dependency or the necessity of the local Church of England bishop. Helwys utilized the logic of the king by asking him if he would consider "it a most cruel tyranny of the king should be by force compelled to understand and believe the scriptures as the hierarchy of Rome would have him, and to worship God and administer in the holy things as the hierarchy would appoint."[83]

The approach assumed that the king would identify with the predicament of those who were being suppressed and persecuted by the Church of England. Thus Helwys asked, "What does it profit the king's people to have

---

81. Ibid., 37.

82. Haymes, "On Religious Liberty," 202.

83. Helwys, *Mystery of Iniquity*, 43.

the Word of God to hear, and read it, seeing they are debarred of the Spirit of God to understand it, but according to private interpretation, by the lord bishops as though they had the Spirit and could not err?"[84] This was the same practice of the first beast. The second beast followed the pattern of the first beast and had now become a suppressor of truth at the expense of the knowledge of God. "But we beseech our lord the king that it may be lawful, without offense to the king, to try the hierarchy on the first ground, which is, that as the hierarchy of Rome says in words they cannot err, that so in their deeds this hierarchy do absolutely profess they cannot err."[85] Helwys demonstrated the connection to the first and second beast by their theological connection. Thus, the Church of England now persecuted the dissenting church via a hierarchy that did not allow dissent of interpretation.

Helwys made an attempt to appeal to the king on the basis of scriptural referent. He made another appeal to the king as ruler of the welfare of the people.

Helwys appealed to the king as a loyal subject by stating that the Church of England had forced loyal English subjects to leave their prince.

> But to pull men that are contrary minded out of their houses by pursuivants, to cast them into prison and cause them to be there at excessive charges, utterly undoing them, their wives, and children, and bringing them to all outward misery, and causing them to be banished from under their natural prince (to whom they are most true subjects), forth of their native country, and from their father's homes and all their friends and familiars.[86]

This above was done by the Church of England on the basis that no English citizen had the right to interpret the Scriptures for him/herself. Barrie White commented that "Helwys's fundamental argument is two-pronged: the king had no right to impose any particular form of religion on the land, and the bishops had no right to claim that theirs should have a monopoly."[87] The situation in England meant that loyal English citizens were forced into prison or banishment in order to serve God per his or her own conscience.

Helwys anticipated the objection to his argument by revealing the disposition of the king should he allow the Scriptures to be interpreted privately and thus settle ecclesiastical disputes. Would the king be held

---

84. Ibid.
85. Ibid., 50–51.
86. Ibid., 44.
87. White, "Early Baptist Arguments," 5.

responsible for the souls of the people should they embrace a deficient interpretation? Helwys did not phrase the issue as such, but he did address the issue:

> Then if men err, their sin shall be upon their own heads, and the king's hand shall be innocent and clear from their transgression, which it cannot be if the king shall willingly suffer his power to be used to compel men to pray and understand by the direction of the lord bishops' spirit . . . And can our lord the king's hand be innocent herein when by the king's power men shall be compelled to sin?[88]

The innocence of the king could not be maintained if he used his power (and sword) to compel men to conformity of worship. He would be guilty of causing his subjects to sin before God. However, should he grant freedom of worship, he would not be responsible for any errors that his subjects might embrace.

Helwys extended this argument to various religions. He argued that "for men's religion to God is between God and themselves. The king shall not answer for it. Neither may the king be judge between God and man. Let them be heretics, Turks, Jews, or whatsoever, it appertains not to the earthly power to punish them in the least measure."[89] Thus, religious freedom was sought for all people without preference for their religion.

Spiritual Bondage and Conscience

The crux of the issue was that, under the authority of Christ, a person possessed the freedom to interpret the Scriptures without the forced coercion of any spiritual authority. Helwys viewed the forced interpretation of Scripture as tantamount to spiritual bondage: "Thus may our lord the king see how his people's spirits are in bondage to the lord bishops' spirit in the understanding of scriptures. And they must of force against their conscience understand them as they command or else go to prison."[90] In order to avoid physical prison, one was forced to enslave oneself in spiritual prison by accepting a false interpretation of the Scriptures.

The gravity of the situation was that Helwys realized that true reform could not exist when conviction of the conscience was suppressed. "But

---

88. Helwys, *Mystery of Iniquity*, 44–45.

89. Ibid., 53.

90. Ibid., 47.

these lord bishops cannot in any wise endure ones that do faithfully seek for reformation, because such are only adversaries to their kingdom."[91] The Church of England could not tolerate those who were reform-minded as the reform itself would denounce the second beast. The end result was that the king, through the Church of England, had now become the persecutor of the loyal dissenters.

Helwys argued that the king could not coerce religious conformity as he was not the judge of man's conscience. "For we do freely profess that our lord the king has no more power over their conscience than over ours, and this none at all."[92] Helwys equated the king's inability to have power of the conscience with the actions of Queen Mary who attempted to force worship but failed. He wrote:

> Our Lord the king will easily see that as Queen Mary by her sword of justice had no power over her subject's consciences (for then had she the power to make them all Papists, and all that resisted her therein suffered justly as evil doers) neither has our lord the king by that sword of justice power over his subject's consciences.[93]

The historical comparison between King James and Queen Mary was hard to miss. Mary could not force those whose conscience had convicted them to worship in a false church. Thus, King James could not compel worship if the individual conscience convicted otherwise.

Should the king have continued to demand worship within the Church of England at the expense of one's conscience, the results would have been that the king caused his own subjects to sin. Helwys wrote:

> It is spiritual obedience that the Lord requires and the king's sword cannot smite the spirits of men. And if our lord the king shall force and compel men to worship and eat the Lord's Supper against their consciences, so shall he make his poor subjects to worship and eat unworthily, whereby he shall compel them to sin against God, and increase their own judgments.[94]

The force of Helwys's statement was sobering for the king. If he were to continue to force the Church of England as the normative for worship, then the result would be that the consciences of the people had sinned against the

---

91. Ibid., 53.
92. Ibid.
93. Ibid., 35.
94. Ibid., 37.

Lord. Thus, the better way for the king to absolve himself from any sin, and at the same time not to be the cause of a personal sin of false worship, was to grant religious freedom to all who dissented based upon their conviction of conscience.

Magistrates and Church Membership

Helwys did not mention the role of the magistrate and church membership specifically, but he did build his case on the concept that a magistrate can be a church member. When Helwys addressed the king as a subject within the spiritual kingdom, that could only mean that he had adopted the mindset that a magistrate can be a church member without rejecting or denouncing his/her standing as a civil servant.

Precisely on this issue, Helwys appealed to the king as a member of the spiritual kingdom when he wrote, "The king must needs grant that as he is an earthly king he can have no power to rule in this spiritual kingdom of Christ, nor can compel any to be subjects thereof, as a king, *while the king is but a subject himself.*"[95] The rationale was that the king possessed jurisdiction outside the church, though not inside the church, as he served under Christ the King. That being stated, the earthly king was subservient to King Jesus and has no warrant "to make primates, metropolitans, archbishops, and lord bishops to be lords in the kingdom of Christ and over the heritage of God."[96] The rationale for this was that the king was a "subject of Christ's kingdom."[97]

Helwys argued that the citizen's responsibility was to know where the kingdom of Caesar and Christ intersected. "For we profess ourselves bound upon the peril of our souls to be faithful subjects both to Jesus Christ our King and to our lord and king. And therefore it stands us upon to know what belongs unto Christ our heavenly king and unto our earthly king."[98]

For Helwys, the conscience serving Jesus based upon the conviction of the Word meant that the earthly king did not possess the right to insist upon compelled religion. Per Helwys, the king certainly had a right to reign over the land and render decisions that impacted society at-large. The extent of the king's jurisdiction was prohibited, however, when it came to

95. Ibid., 39; emphasis mine.
96. Ibid.
97. Ibid.
98. Ibid., 40.

matters of conscience, as the king was a member of the spiritual kingdom. However, should the king have failed to understand this position and compel worship, then the earthly king would have replaced the heavenly king. Helwys questioned the rationale for this action. "For what greater evil can be committed against Christ than to take his honor and power from him and give it to earthly men, who should fear and tremble before him in giving to him glory and honor and not taking from him?"[99] Forced worship by an earthly king would be tantamount to having one rule over another in the spiritual kingdom, which was forbidden by the Lord.

The end result of Helwys's argument was that he recognized a godly king. Helwys desired the godly king to be a part of the spiritual kingdom and not the leader of the spiritual kingdom as that right was reserved for Christ. The king then must be one of many church members who have freedom in Christ along with the responsibility to serve Christ in the church. For Helwys, the king and magistrates had a place in Baptist ecclesiology, but a limited place nonetheless.

Implications for Baptist Ecclesiology

In the Mystery of Iniquity, Thomas Helwys advocated the limited use of the sword for civil affairs only. He rejected the use of the sword as a means to resolve ecclesiastical problems. Helwys utilized the scriptural method of dealing with sin and rebellion through excommunication.

A Declaration of Faith of the English People Remaining at Amsterdam

Articles 17 and 18 of this work reveal a developed ecclesiology that dealt with internal problems from a biblical basis rather than from a civil platform. Article 17 states,

> That Brethren impenitent in one sin after the admonition off the Church, are to bee excluded the communion off the Sainets. Mat. 18.17. 1 Cor. 5.4, 13. & therefore not the committing off sin doth cut off anie from the Church, but refusing to heare the Church to reformacion.[100]

99. Ibid.

100. Helwys, "Declaration of Faith," 121.

The concept expressed was that the believer, even though unrepentant, was to remain unharmed by the sword. The church was to treat the unrepentant believer as one who no longer enjoyed the fellowship of the church. Sin was not be tolerated by the church body. On the other hand, sin was not to be punished by a government-appointed magistrate.

Article 18 referred to the excommunicant and civil relations within society. "That Excommunicants in respect of civil societie are not to bee avoided, 2 Thess. 3.15. Mat. 18.17."[101] Helwys had thoroughly pronounced a division between the sacred and the secular. The church possessed the scriptural command to deal with the sinful person, but did not have scriptural warrant to treat the excommunicant as a heathen in civil affairs. Thus, Helwys worked through the relationship between the use of the sword and the use of spiritual means to correct a sinful member.

The role of the magistrate, for instance civil authorities, in the Baptist church was a distinguishing position firmly understood to lie between the Mennonites, who completely shunned the magistrate, and the Church of England that was thoroughly magisterial in its reform via Royal Supremacy. Article 24 reads:

> That Magistracy is a Holy ordinance of God, that every soul ought to be subject to it for fear only, but for conscience sake. Magistrates are the ministers of God for our wealth, they bear the sword for nought. They are ministers of God to take vengeance on them that do evil, Rom. 13. That it is fearful sin to speak evil of them that are in dignity, and to despise Government. 2 Pet 2:10. That we are to pray for them, for God would have them saved and come to the knowledge of his truth. 1 Tim 2:1–4. And therefore they may be members of the Church of Christ retaining their Magistracy, for no Holy Ordinance of God debars any from being a member of Christ's Church. They beare the sword off God,—which sword in all Lawful administracions is to bee defended and supported by the servants off God that are vnder their Government with their lyves and al that they have according as in the first Institucion off that Holie Ordinance. And whosoever holds otherwise must hold, (iff they vnderstad themselves) that they are the ministers of the devil, and therefore not to bee praied for nor approved in anie off their adminstracions,—seing all things they do (as punishing offenders and defending their countries, state, and persons by the sword) is vnlawful. [102]

101. Ibid.

102. Ibid., 122–23.

To conclude that Helwys was directing this comment toward the Mennonites who rejected civil servants as church members is easy. However, the consequence of this statement is that church membership, in a Baptist church, was open to all believers without regard to vocation or civil community standing. Basically, this meant that the social structure of the church was defined by one's standing before God and not one's status in the community.

Additionally, Article 24 served to advance the possible ministry of the church within English society. According to the Mennonites, magistrates could not be members of the church. Helwys advanced the cause of Baptist ecclesiology by ministering to those who were magistrates. In this area, he distanced Baptist ecclesiology from the Mennonite Anabaptists. William R. Estep comments on this issue:

> This article was exceedingly important. It articulated a far more positive attitude toward the state than either Smyth or the Mennonites expressed. Once Baptists were distinguished from Anabaptists, this position alone would give their movement not only chances of survival but also the possibility of influencing society through an active participation in government which the Mennonites had never enjoyed.[103]

This position allowed Helwys to address the *Mystery of Iniquity* to King James, because he took the position that Baptists could participate in government and perhaps influence policy for the better.

An Advertisement or Admonition unto the Congregations, Which Men Call the New Frylers, in the Lowe Countries

In his work, *An Advertisement or Admonition unto the Congregations, Which Men Call the New Frylers, in the Lowe Countries*,[104] Helwys expanded upon his concept of the magistracy and church membership. This work was written in 1611 to "repudiate several Waterlander doctrines that had been embraced by John Smyth."[105] Helwys presented the position "that the king, prince, and magistrates, ruling and governing by the power of God with the sword of justice may be members of the church of Christ while retaining

103. Estep, "Bold Architect," 30.
104. Helwys, *Advertisement or Admonition unto the Congregations*.
105. Ibid., 93.

the magistracy."[106] Helwys argued that the apostle Paul (Rom 13:1–7) commended the use of the sword for the benefit of society as ordained by God.

When Helwys sent his copy of *Mystery of Iniquity* to King James, he had already thought through the membership requirements of the Baptist church. He concluded that the Bible did not limit membership based upon vocation, for instance, any English civil magistrate could join a Baptist church if they were saved. By pronouncing magistrates as being worthy of membership, he denounced those who misunderstood the position of the magistrate. In fact, he stated that if one should reject magistrates for membership, they must understand that they had concluded magistrates were workers of the devil. This position went against the fact that magistrates were also appointed by God to serve society at-large. By appealing to the king, Helwys was recognizing the authority of the king and the English magistrates, welcoming them into the Baptist church, but limiting their role to that of servant and not ruler. Thus, magistrates ruled in civil society, but only one ruler existed in Baptist ecclesiology—King Jesus.

The role of conscience and religious liberty was the foundation from which Helwys wrote the *Mystery of Iniquity*. The entire work was predicated upon the conviction that Baptists and all men should have the freedom to worship God without fear of reprisal from an earthly government. Helwys presented the radical case that an individual could be members to two kingdoms (earthly and spiritual) without exhibiting disloyalty to either. Helwys's concept of religious freedom was a radical departure of the accepted norm concerning church-and-state relations. During the seventeenth century, the prevailing idea was that a nation could not be unified unless its religion was the same. Timothy George recognizes the demarcation of church and state relations that Helwys advanced. He comments:

> Despite their protestations of civil loyalty, the Baptists advanced a view of the relation of church and state which could only be considered revolutionary in early Stuart England. They advocated the complete separation of temporal and spiritual realms, the disestablishment of religion, and the uninhibited toleration of all religious sects and opinions.[107]

Helwys presented the idea that citizenship and loyalty to the earthly king was a command of God, and as such, God's commands were conducive to God's work in the Baptist *ecclesia*.

106. Ibid., 129.

107. George, "Between Pacifism and Coercion," 3–49.

Baptist Ecclesiology Considered

Helwys provided an alternative to Magisterial Reformed churches. In the Baptist church model, the path was open to working with civil magistrates as authentic members, but not being governed by them. This concept was unheard of in Helwys's day. Laying the foundation that civil servants could be a member of a Baptist *ecclesia* allowed Helwys to address the deviant position of the Puritans. Their attempts to reform a false church gave Helwys the freedom to present his case for Baptist ecclesiology in the hope they would understand biblical *ecclesia*. This issue will be the focus of the next chapter.

5

Helwys's Critique of Puritanism

Introduction

THOMAS HELWYS BEGINS BOOK III by addressing the Puritans. The issue at stake for Helwys is the Puritans were a part of the Church of England and desired to reform the national church. From the Puritans' point of view, the benefits of such reform meant that they could stay in good standing with the crown by adherence to royal supremacy, have the honor of English citizenship, and embrace Protestant theology.

Helwys realized that, from an ecclesiological position, Baptists had moved beyond Puritanism and the Church of England. Where the Puritans sought to reform a corrupt church, the Baptists took the position that restoration of the church could be the only alternative. Per Helwys, the Church of England was categorized as the Second Beast and, thus, purifying the national church was not possible.

This chapter will review the rise of Puritanism, the basic tenets of Reformed Covenant Theology as they relate to Ecclesiology, and the rationale for purifying the Church of England. The chapter will progress to Helwys's denunciation of the Puritan movement as a deficient ecclesiological system as compared to Baptist ecclesiology.

The Rise of Puritanism

The rise of Puritanism is not easily ascertained. Leonard J. Trinterud articulates the position that Puritanism is "the heritage from medieval English thought and life."[1] He continues on to say that Puritanism was "indigenous, not exotic, to England."[2] Patrick Collinson made the claim that the name Puritan "took over as the brand name for a certain kind of Protestant religiosity, social conduct and politics was indeed a defining moment in English culture."[3] The English culture disliked the Independents of the seventeenth century, so the term "Puritan" may have "originated with exiled Catholic polemicists who found this reference to ancient perfectionist heresies a convenient target with which to brush the Elizabethan Protestant establishment."[4]

Collinsons's connection of English life to English Puritanism means that the dating of the Puritan movement can be placed before the reign of Queen Elizabeth. B. R. White concurs with Collinson and Trinterud as he writes that early separatist tradition of thought existed before Robert Browne in the "London Protestant Congregation in Queen Mary's days."[5] White goes on to make the case that "the Separatists were always to stand close to those of their less radical brethren who remained, albeit sometimes rather precariously, within the outward communion of the Church of England."[6]

Even though White discusses the emergence of Separatism, he unites both the more radical Separatists with the less radical Puritans by connecting their disdain for the Church of England. Doing so allows a common ecclesiology that wanted reform at an early date. The beginnings of Puritanism/Separatism seem to be early during the reign of Queen Mary. More concisely, Trinterud points to the reign of Queen Mary for the emergence of Puritanism.[7] Christiana Garrett concurs with this assessment as she

1. Trinturd, "Origins of Puritanism," 37.

2. Ibid.

3. Collinson, "Antipuritanism," 23.

4. Ibid., 19.

5. White, *English Separatist Tradition*, 32.

6. Ibid., 32–33. The context makes the case clear that White is referring to Puritans when he references them as being less radical.

7. Trinterud states that "Puritanism emerged in Tudor England in the thought and work of men such as William Tyndale, John Frith, John Bale, John Hooper, John Bradford, and their associates." See Trinterud, "Origins of Puritanism," 38. Using the

writes, "we are dealing with the embryo of the Puritan party, both clerical and lay. Here they worked out their worship practices and political agenda using the opportunity of exile to organize themselves into a formidable opposition party."[8]

Even though the seeds of thought were imbedded early in the Tudor reign, the actual event that served as the catalyst for the Puritan movement to gain momentum was the reaction against the 1559 Revised Common Prayer Book and vestments for the clergy. Griswold comments:

> They objected to vestments, which represented a reversion to popery, and thought that the 1559 Revised Prayer Book reverted to the ornaments of the 1549 Prayer Book. They promoted, in its stead, the use of the Genevan Bible, and John Fox's *Acts and Monuments*, which characterized the Roman Catholic Church as an instrument of AntiChrist.[9]

The Puritans did not like the resemblance of worship of the Church of England. For them, it was still closely akin to Roman Catholicism. Consequently, the Puritans did not accept the reform agenda of Queen Elizabeth.

Patrick Collinson is more sympathetic to the Queen as a person and to the political forces at work during the Queen's reign. First his comments about the Queen are in order.

> Queen Elizabeth's church policy was not unaffected by her private religious opinions, which seem to have been those of a moderate protestant, held with the independence of a mind which was not possessed by any of the current orthodoxies . . . But with Elizabeth, the queen often obscures the believer as well as the woman, and her conduct of church affairs was above all an act of statesmanship.[10]

Per Collinson, Elizabeth's professional demeanor helped the political situation in England as it was volatile.

Concerning the political situation during her reign, Collinson goes on to state that Elizabeth was attempting to unify her country.

---

dates of John Bale, the possibility emerges that, while a refugee on the main Continent, time allowed him (and many others) to develop Puritan ideas and import them back to England during the reign of Queen Elizabeth. This does not mean a full-fledged Puritan position was developed, but it does allow the possibility that the fledging ecclesiology of both Puritanism and Separatism was emerging.

8. Garrett, *Marian Exiles*, 40. I am indebted to Barbara Griswold for the quote.

9. Griswold, "Congregational Dynamics," 24.

10. Collinson, *Elizabethan Puritan Movement*, 29.

She succeeded to a kingdom which contained sharply opposed religious interests which, for all that they were both minority interests, threatened political division and social disturbance. Moreover, the country was so weak externally that its viability as an independent state was open to question. In these circumstances expediency dictated a religious policy which would cause the minimum of offense to a Europe where the great powers had rejected the Reformation, and one which would hold out some hope of healing rather than exacerbating domestic divisions. Historians have always agreed that these considerations governed Elizabeth's approach to a church settlement rather than those which the returning exiles commended to her attention.[11]

Elizabeth was trying to avert war with Europe, appease the English Catholic constituency, and move the Church of England in a Protestant direction. Her task was monumental but much to her credit she slowly directed the church and country to a Protestant agenda.

Puritan Opposition

The objection of the Puritans was met with the queen's determination to force conformity to the royal agenda. The issue of preaching licensure became volatile for the Puritans. In fact, Champlin Burrage states the issue of license brought about the change in nomenclature for the Puritans. Burrage states:

> It cannot have been long after March, 1565, that the Nonconformist ministers who had lost their licenses to preach began to try to find a way out of their difficulties. About this time (1566?) the name Puritan first appears in English literature. Bishop Grindal in a letter to Henry Bullinger, dated London, Aug. 27, 1566, says, "It is scarcely credible how much this controversy about things of no importance [i.e., the vestments, etc.] has disturbed our churches, and still, in great measure, continues to do. . . ."[12]

The fact that the Puritans could not officially preach, but made a contentious issue over the issue of vestments and license earned them the title of Puritans.

---

11. Ibid., 29–30.
12. Burrage, *Early English Dissenters*, 79.

Edwin C. Deibler additionally comments that the Puritans objected to the vestments. He states:

> These men objected to much of the ceremonialism carried over into the Elizabethan church from the medieval church; they objected to the vestments worn by the clergy. They had little use for any religion which was mainly ceremonial. . . . Puritans might disagree among themselves on the degree of ceremonialism they might be content to retain in their public worship, but they concurred in the conviction that the outward ritual was a secondary matter; religion was for them primarily an affair of the heart.[13]

The Puritans were not content with the ceremonies of the Church of England as they were reminders of Roman Catholicism which, in Puritan thought, possessed an outward focus. In the Puritan mind, Roman Catholicism did not impact the inner man, but rather remained ceremonial in scope.

The problem of licensed preachers was complicated by the fact that so many who were licensed were simply not capable of preaching. Morgan states:

> Elizabeth's new bishops had filled vacant benefices with incompetent and disreputable men, unqualified to preach the gospel while able but intransigent Puritan preachers were rejected and silenced. Puritans set much store by preaching, which they considered the principal means ordained by God for instructing people in the great truth revealed by the Scriptures. . . . Puritans therefore resented the appointment of ministers who were unable or unfit to instruct their congregations by preaching.[14]

Per the Puritan mindset, the hearts of men could not be instructed by parish priests with Roman Catholic vestments, who were uneducated or unskilled in preaching. Their license did not improve their abilities, but only legalized them as unfit parish ministers. Thus, the Puritans wanted nothing more than to purify the Church of England with a reform that was biblically based.

Recent scholarship by Collinson has contradicted the position of Morgan and Trinterud.

> Within their dioceses, archdeaconries and parishes they were often free to apply a generously protestant interpretation to the

---

13. Deibler, "Chief Characteristic of Early English Puritanism," 331–32.
14. Morgan, *Visible Saints*, 7.

queen's ecclesiastical policy and to obscure what may seem to us the true essence of Anglicanism as the Elizabethan settlement defined it. Preaching went forward—far more of it than Elizabeth ever thought desirable—and the Prayer Book was allowed to become the vehicle of a simplified puritan worship. For much of the time and in many localities it must have seemed that puritan aspirations would be satisfied without schism and even without conspicuous conflict.[15]

Collinson argues that much of the Church of England was defined by Puritan preaching. The English Reform was moving along the lines of a Puritan agenda.

Puritan Ecclesiology

The dissatisfaction with the Church of England did not mean that the Puritans desired to separate from the national church. For the Puritan movement, Reform meant to stay part of the church in order to change from within. The rationale was that the reform established by King Henry was a start toward Protestantism, but Henrican, Edwardian, and Elizabethan reform attempts were incomplete. The Church of England was still a resemblance of Roman Catholicism.

The validity of that issue did not go unnoticed by Thomas Helwys in Book III. Helwys called the Church of England a false reform. He states:

> You testify hereby against yourselves that you are unreformed, and that there is a way of reformation, wherein you would be, if you might have leave or license to enter thereinto, which seeing you cannot obtain, you justify it lawful to walk in an unreformed profession of religion upon this ground because you may not have leave by act of Parliament to reform. . . . Let this suffice in this place to prove that you walk in a false profession of Christ by your own acknowledgement, calling daily for liberty that you might reform yourselves, but seeing it will not be granted, you go on in the false way you disapprove of.[16]

The argument is that the Puritans knew what true reform should be as they called for it to be implemented. This indictment of the Puritans is revealing in that the Puritans knew that they did not have reform, even though the

---

15. Collinson, *Elizabethan Puritan Movement*, 59–60.

16. Helwys, *Mystery of Iniquity*, 64–65.

Church of England was a reformed church. Per the Puritans, the reform was simply not thorough, and Helwys used their own position against them.

The second implication with which Helwys charges the Puritans is that their reform was only capable if the King granted reform. Thus, a spiritual reform was impossible unless the heart of the King, which was unresponsive to Puritans, was changed toward them. For the Puritan, the spiritual authority was, in a very practical sense, still vested in the temporal King. Thus, the Puritans desired a church-state ecclesiology.

The third implication of Helwys is that true reform would be thorough and would recognize that a church-state ecclesiology is unbiblical. True reform would embrace Baptist ecclesiology that the rightful head of the church is not a human government, but rather a divine government with Jesus Christ as its head.

Tenets of Puritan Ecclesiology[17]

The Church of England was the result of political reform. Puritans realized the pitfalls of such an attempt. James Coggins comments on the political issue of English Reformation:

> The English Reformation consisted of two parts: an act of state in which the English king replaced the pope as the head of the Church of England, and a more widespread religious revolution in which Catholic theology and practice were replaced by Protestant theology and practice. . . . There were also Puritans, who were influenced by the writings and teachings of John Calvin and other continental theologians of the Reformed tradition.[18]

Coggins goes on to say:

> They wanted to shape the Church of England on Reformed lines: Bible based preaching in place of liturgy and the elaborate celebration of the Lord's Supper; Presbyterian rather than Episcopal church government; a stronger church vis-à-vis the state; the teaching of predestination; and more rigid moral standards. Like the continental Reformed, they attempted to reform the church from within.[19]

17. This section of the book will only survey the most basic tenets of Puritan ecclesiology. It is not intended to be an exhaustive treatment of the subject matter.

18. Coggins, *John Smyth's Congregation*, 29.

19. Ibid.

The Puritans wanted reform that mirrored the continental reform. The issue of a reformed national church was foremost in the minds of the Puritans. Based upon the church-state model present in continental Europe, they believed that reform was possible. Morgan concurs when he writes, "their aim was to gain control of the existing government and through the government to reform the church."[20]

National Church

The paradigm of the state-church was embedded in the reform efforts of Europe to the extent that any thought of challenging the paradigm was considered absurd at best and heretical at worst. This simply meant that reform had to take place with governmental approval. Puritans were content to allow Parliament to change the direction of the church. However, that change never happened to the satisfaction for Puritan reform. White comments:

> Yet gradually, painfully, and most unwillingly, the advanced Protestants, the men soon to be labeled "Puritans," whose ideal of the Church was Genevan rather than Episcopalian, were to learn that, in ecclesiastical matters as in much else, the Queen was herself an unbending conservative. . . . For perhaps the first half of her reign it was Elizabeth's will, and virtually her will alone, which blocked the policies of her more advanced Protestant subjects.[21]

The Puritans attempted to work the political process in order to bring about reform. The attempt failed and reform, per the Puritan movement, did not occur.

In 1572, the Puritans presented a document entitled *Admonition to Parliament*, which asked for liturgical and doctrinal reforms to be enacted by Parliament.[22] The move was legal in scope, but it also had more far-reaching legal ramifications. Trinterud comments:

> This move struck hard in two directions. It assumed that Parliament had full authority to make these changes. The argument was that since Parliament had instituted the settlement of religious

20. Morgan, *Visible Saints*, 16.

21. White, *English Separatist Tradition*, 21.

22. Craig, "The Growth of English Puritanism," 39. Craig describes the *Admonition* "as an anonymous composite manifesto . . . an indictment especially of the government of the Reformed Church of England that pulled no punches and became an instant bestseller."

affairs upon which Elizabeth was then acting, it also had power to alter this settlement. In the second place it called for an organization of the Church upon the basis of a series of representative church courts elected by the people. Such a system would make impossible any control of the Church by Elizabeth or the bishops.[23]

Inadvertently, the result was a solidly based church-state union. However, the Puritans thought that the union would be controlled by Parliament, but it only strengthened the Crown's position of royal supremacy.

The approach to change the form of the reform but keep the church as a national church created two opposing factions within the Church of England, for instance, those who were Anglican and those who were Puritan. Quoting and paraphrasing John Coolidge, Richard L. Greaves reviews the difference between the two groups.

> The case for demarcating "Anglicans" and Puritans in theological terms is further buttressed by the research of John Coolidge, whose fundamental premise is that "Puritanism must be defined in the first instance by contradistinction from Anglican Conformity, and historically the 'chief and principal ground' of intellectual difference between Conformists and Puritans concerns the appeal to Scriptural authority." Puritans had to have positive reinforcement from Scripture; a thing had to be "according to the Word of God, whereas, it was sufficient for 'Anglicans' that something be 'not against' the Bible."[24]

The Puritans wanted assurance that reform was scriptural. Therefore, they were discontented with any resemblance of the Roman Church as being part of the Church of England. Yet, neither were they of the mindset to leave the national church. Again, Greaves explains:

> The key to "the whole mystery of Elizabethan Puritanism," according to Coolidge, was the Puritan's belief that indifferent things (*adiaphora*) had to be used to edify. For the Puritan, edification created order in the church, whereas for "Anglican" edification took place once order had been established, especially by regulating indifferent things. Thus for the "Anglican" the church was an established, nonliving institution, while for the Puritan it was a living body. To separate from the Church of England was, in

---

23. Trinterud, "Origins of Puritanism," 47.
24. Greaves, "Puritan-Nonconformist Tradition in England," 459.

Puritan eyes, tantamount to destroying a living body and was thus unacceptable.[25]

Even though the Church of England needed thorough reform, the Puritans considered it to be a church that was viable as a living body of Christ and worthy of reform attempts. They did not consider their church as part of Rome but as an emerging national Protestant church in England.

Covenant Theology

The concept of covenant has a long history within Christianity.[26] The Puritan's use of covenant theology became prominent during the reign of Edward VI. Trinterud attributes the fact "that the covenant scheme became fixed in English theology" was a direct result of the "famous Rhineland leaders, Peter Martyr, Bucer, Tremellius (a converted Jewish Hebraist of great ability), Fagius, Dryander, and others."[27]

Puritan covenantal theology understood a divine movement was present, at God's initiative, in securing the relationship with humanity and then the subsequent movement of humanity to enter the relationship based upon soteriology. Jerald C. Brauer states:

> The objective was preserved in the structuring of God's initiative in a definite form, but the subjective was protected in that man had to enter this relationship personally through an experience of forgiveness and faith. The rationale was preserved in that a man living under the covenant lived according to God's law as originally written in the heart and as present in the structure of nature's law. The emotional was equally preserved in that the ability to live under the covenant was dependent upon constant incursions of God's Spirit stirring up man's zeal.[28]

The concept of God's taking the initiative to form a relationship with humanity was connected to the natural law that God structured in the created order. However, no covenant language is found in the created order.

25. Ibid.

26. The review of the history of covenant theology is beyond the scope of the book. However, one source is Trinterud's article, which has been cited. It is a concise article that reveals the history of covenant theology and its popularity for the English Puritans.

27. Trinterud, "Origins of Puritanism," 44. The Rhineland reformers were more concerned with natural law than with predestination.

28. Brauer, "Nature of English Puritanism," 104.

Covenant theology notes that the *protoevangelium* and the covenant made with Noah are valid.[29]

The problem lies in the fact of how covenant theology avoids universalism if soteriology is based upon the previous covenants. This fact required covenant theologians to embrace the Abrahamic covenant as the logical solution for the election of a specific people to be redeemed. Thus, universalism was avoided, and the covenant concept was established.

The emphasis of the Abrahamic covenant is that God obligated himself to fulfill the covenant by calling Abraham to be his representative to build a great nation of people. The prophetic issue of the Abrahamic covenant found fulfillment in Jesus Christ. "Moreover, in the incarnation, death and resurrection of Christ God did actually fulfill that promise to which his covenant bound him. Therefore, the sacraments are witnesses, attestations, or seals to the effect that God has long since fulfilled his covenant, his promise."[30]

A brief explanation of Puritan and Separatist definitions for the word "covenant" is warranted. Trinterud gives the position there were actually two meanings with two applications of the word "covenant" among the English Puritans. The first meaning adopted by the nonconforming Presbyterians was that covenant meant "a promise given laterally and unconditionally by God to his elect." This is primarily the pattern that the Puritans embraced as they stayed within the Church of England.

However, the Separatists utilized another meaning more akin to the Rhineland reformers. Covenant was not so much a promise, but more of a contract between parties. Thus, the Separatists could logically conclude that the Church of England was not founded upon covenant as magistrates had established it. However, the Puritans understood covenant to be God working with the elect nation of England. According to Paul Christiansen, the Puritans knew that the problems in the Church of England needed more reform, but they equated the Church of England with the Laodicea church. In other words, the Church of England was a true biblical church that needed leadership or magistrates to complete the reform.[31]

The differences in the definitions became substantial in terms of a true visible church. The Puritans acknowledged that the Church of England

29. Trinterud, "Origins of Puritanism," 42.

30. Ibid., 45. The discussion and meaning of baptism will take place in chapter 6 with the review of the different positions of Separatism and Baptist.

31. Christiansen, *Reformers and Babylon*, 9–11.

was a flawed but true church, whereas Separatists denounced the national church as corrupt in its inception. Therefore, in order to restore the true church, separation was the solution.

The Puritans embraced William Tyndale's concept that Israel was called to be God's people and, thus, had the responsibility of reform. Tyndale differed with Martin Luther in that the Law was still operative and relevant.[32] Thus, the Puritans followed John Foxe that England was a chosen nation. They followed John Calvin in that they laid the doctrine of predestination over the existing Deuteronomist grid inherited from William Tyndale. James C. Spalding comments, "England's saga continued Israel's saga. Through Foxe's book English people could discern judgment and grace in the events of their history and on the basis of that history discern the signs of judgment and grace in their own times."[33] Thus, national identity embraced by a national reformed church, fostered by a hermeneutic identity with Israel, was the Puritan approach to reform in the Church of England.

Paul S. Fiddes argues that covenant actually had four meanings. The first meaning is "covenant referred to an eternal 'covenant of grace' which God has made with human beings." The second meaning is "the divine covenant could refer to a transaction between the persons of the triune God, in which the Son is envisaged as consenting to the will of the Father to undertake the work of salvation for the elect." Fiddes presents the third meaning as "an agreement which God makes corporately with his church, or with particular churches." The fourth meaning of covenant is more anthropocentric. "That is 'covenant' can refer to the agreement undertaken and signed by church members when a particular local church was founded, and subsequently by new members on entering it."[34]

The concept of covenant was theologically developing in the minds of the Puritans which precluded a static meaning. At various times each of the above definitions were utilized as the ecclesiological emphasis of the covenant was given attention. The key theological feature was the eternal nature of the covenant and its relationship to the church.

---

32. The scope of work for the book does not allow an historic review of William Tyndale's works to ferret out all the historic impact upon the Puritans. For a concise review of this position, see Spalding, "Restitution as a Normative Factor for Puritan Dissent," 47–63.

33. Ibid., 54.

34. Fiddes, *Tracks and Traces*, 25–29.

Visible and Invisible Church

The Puritans followed Augustine in the function of the church. The Augustinian model rejected the Donatist model, which required purity in the lives of the saints as the litmus test for a true church.[35] A brief review of the Donatist controversy is described:

> The Donatists were a schismatic body in the African Church who became divided from the Catholics through their refusal to accept Caecilian, Bishop of Carthage on the ground that his consecrator, Felix of Aptunga, had been a *traditor* during the Diocletianic persecution. . . . Theologically the Donatists were rigorists, holding that the Church of the saints must remain "holy" and the sacraments conferred by *traditores* were invalid. Apart from their denial that Felix of Aptunga was in fact a *traditor*, the Church maintained that the unworthiness of the minister did not affect the validity of sacraments, since, as Augustine insisted, their true minister was Christ. The Donatists, on the other hand, went so far as to assert that all those who communicated with *traditores* were infected, and that, since the Church is one and holy, the Donatists alone formed the Church.[36]

The Donatists' emphasis on the purity of the Church was not lost on the Puritans. The Donatists maintained that, if the church was impure, then it is incumbent upon the true church to depart and embrace purity and reject the worldly that is within the church. Sin affected the entire body; therefore, in order to save the church, separation was the only viable alternative.

However, the Puritans followed Augustine's approach to dealing with sin within the church by adopting the visible/invisible ecclesiological concept. Augustine did address the Donatists' concerns about the giving and receiving of the sacraments. In the process, though, he revealed his concept of ecclesiology. Augustine stated:

> So let them understand that men may be baptized in communions severed from the Church, in which Christ's baptism is given and received in the said celebration of the sacrament, but that it will only then be of avail for the remission of sins, when the recipient, being reconciled to the unity of the Church, is purged from

---

35. Unfortunately, the historic review of the Donatist Controversy will not be exhaustive, as the issue is not the main concern of this chapter.

36. Cross and Livingston, *Oxford Dictionary of the Christian Church*, s.v. "Donatism."

the sacrilege of deceit, by which his sins were retained, and their remission prevented.[37]

Augustine maintained the position that forgiveness of sins was only found in the official established church. Baptism could be administered by a heretic, but the benefit of baptism could only be experienced in connection with the true church. Thus, a schism could offer baptism, which is valid, but only effectual for forgiveness of sins if connected with the catholic or universal church.

Augustine's ecclesiology allowed the mixture of those who have known sin with those who are known not to have the same sin. Thus, the possibility exists where a local church could have sinners and saints mixed together in the congregation. In fact Augustine elaborated on that concept in his famous work, *The City of God.* He stated:

> So, too, as long as she is a stranger in the world, the city of God has in her communion, and bound to her by the sacraments, some who shall not eternally dwell in the lot of the saints. Of these, some are not now recognized; others declare themselves, and do not hesitate to make common cause with our enemies in murmuring against God, whose sacramental badge they wear. These men you may today see thronging the churches with us, tomorrow crowding the theatres with the godless. . . . In truth, these two cities are entangled together in this world, and intermixed until the last judgment effects their separation.[38]

The concept of a visible mixed church became a common ecclesiological doctrine from Augustine through the time of the Reformers. The saved and unsaved people who comprised the visible church would coexist until God separated them in the coming future judgment.

The reason for this judgment is that the visible church was not so pure but sinful, whereas, the invisible church was pure. Thus, after the separation, the true church would be known. The issue of course means that the true church existed in the world at the same time as the mixed church, but it was invisible as the hearts of men are known only to God. The only visible means of the church was the mixed church, and the only means of correcting the mixed church was the presentation of discipline and the Word.

The Puritans followed the ecclesiology of Augustine. Morgan concurs by stating, "But some of them did develop a unique conception of church

---

37. Augustine, *On Baptism, against the Donatists* 1.12.18; 4:419.

38. Augustine, *City of God* 1.35; 2:21.

membership, designed to make the visible church a closer approximation of the invisible than St. Augustine probably had in mind."[39]

Summary of Puritan Ecclesiology

The Puritans believed that the constituted Church of England was impure, but nonetheless a valid church. The issue of reform for the Puritans meant that a biblical approach could only occur if connection to the church was maintained. The cement that held the Puritan foundation together was the embrace of covenant theology. Under the headship of their Christian king, the Church of England was the solution to the wickedness of Roman Catholicism.

The fact that the Church of England had a political ruler was not an unbiblical issue, as the covenant theology was predicated upon the continuity between the Old and New Testaments with Israel serving as an example. In covenantal theology, the history of redemption was foundational in the effort to demonstrate grace acting upon the elect of the Old and New Testaments. Michael McGiffert stated, "Covenant theology was thus from the start a theology of history—the history of the chosen people, first Jews, then Christians, to whom God bound himself by promise, oath, and sacramental seal."[40] Thus, Puritan England understood they were a part of God's work, as the English nation was the continuity to God's work between the New Testament church and the Church of England.

Regardless of the political and ecclesiastical problems, Puritans never considered leaving the Church of England. They had embraced the idea that they were the catalyst of thorough reform for their beloved national church. In the Puritan covenantal mindset, the Church of England was constituted on a solid biblical base. Thomas Helwys would challenge the Puritan presupposition.

Thomas Helwys and Puritan Ecclesiology

In Book III, Helwys equated the Puritans with being false prophets. This is a strong charge in that a false prophet pretended to be sent from God, but in actuality was not. Helwys demonstrated that the Puritans did not have

---

39. Morgan, *Visible Saints*, 4.

40. McGiffert, "Grace and Works," 470.

biblical qualifications to be ordained as pastors. He lists the qualifications of 1 Timothy 3 and Titus 1 as the standard for all potential candidates who desired the office of pastor. Those men who could not meet the stringency of the qualifications were not to be considered as pastor. In Helwys's mind, Puritans did not meet the standard biblical qualifications. "For all that are not so, both in themselves and their wives and children, are not sent of God to be pastors of his flock, but are false prophets in the first degree. For God sends none but those that are according to his own rule."[41]

Church Polity: The Puritan Deficiency

The means of calling a pastor is accomplished by the election and ordination of the church. At this point, Helwys displays one of the fundamental differences between the Church of England and Baptist ecclesiology. The local parish priests were appointed by the bishop and the hierarchy of the Church of England.

Helwys knew the history of the Puritan movement. The issue of preaching was a problem in the parish churches. Most Puritans were persuaded that the local pastor was incapable of proclaiming the Word of God. Griswold stated:

> A pressing concern of the Puritans was not only the moral degradation they saw in church and society, but the woeful state of ignorance and error among communicants, due to the lack of preaching and catechizing. . . . This estate of spiritual turpitude was viewed as a result of the incompetence and non-residency of the clerics, a condition foisted upon the parishes by the bishops.[42]

The situation in the Church of England meant that the local parish minister was, in fact, not local. In certain situations, he did not live near the congregation, nor did he relate to them. Thus, in the mind of Helwys, the local minister was a paid hireling. Helwys addressed the issue:

> But to get an election for money, either of a man's own, or of his friends, or by private favor or friendship or beholdings to men, and so corruptly to become a pastor over a flock of people diversely affected, and many openly profane and wicked, here is an unholy election of an unholy pastor over a corrupt and unholy

41. Helwys, *Mystery of Iniquity*, 66.
42. Griswold, "Congregational Dynamics," 26.

> flock. . . . Christ himself has adjudged you all, not to be shepherds
> of the sheep, but to be thieves and robbers. And thus you are all
> false prophets.[43]

The issue of calling a pastor to a local parish was stated in terms that
revealed the depth of the situation. Puritans knew that the local church
should be the deciding factor in the calling of a pastor to a church. To place
that responsibility, along with the authority and privilege to enact such a
monumental decision, in the hands of the hierarchy of the Church of England was evidence that the Church of England in general and the Puritans
in particular were not true churches.

Church Polity: Baptist Congregational Authority

Helwys presented the position that the local church is responsible for elect-
ing and ordaining their own pastor. He wrote:

> And now election and ordination, which is the door and way
> whereby the true bishops and pastors of the flock do enter. The
> Holy Ghost does teach (Acts 14:23) that election and ordination
> were performed in and by the church or congregation with fast-
> ing and prayer. This is the door and way, and all that have entered
> by any other way are thieves and robbers, as our Savior Christ
> testifies (John 10).[44]

The calling or election of a pastor, per Helwys's presentation of Baptist
ecclesiology, was now the responsibility of the congregation. The issue of
congregational authority became one of the identifying characteristics of
the Baptist movement.

Helwys made the case that a holy people (congregation) had the ability to call a godly man who met the biblical qualifications to be their own
pastor. "What a blessed comfort were it for a holy man to be elected of a
holy people."[45] This simply means that a godly congregation could follow
the pastoral leadership of the man they loved and, in the same manner, a
godly pastor would lead the people with the love of Christ. "So should a
godly people have holy pastors over them, and whom they would all love
and reverence. And so should godly pastors have a holy people to follow

---

43. Helwys, *Mystery of Iniquity*, 66.

44. Ibid.

45. Ibid.

them whom they would carefully feed and cherish."[46] Helwys could write this admonition to the Puritans as his position had been delineated in Amsterdam with John Smyth.[47]

Church Polity: Baptist Congregational Development in Amsterdam

A "Short Confession of Faith in XX Articles by John Smyth" was written in 1609.[48] This confession records Smyth's development of Baptist ecclesiology in two primary areas that Helwys expanded upon later. The first development is congregational authority. The second area is the rejection of infant baptism.[49]

Smyth addresses the role of the church as it administers polity. The "Short Confession" addresses the Church in Articles 12–18. In Article 13 Smyth writes: "That the church of Christ has power delegated to themselves of announcing the word, administering the sacraments, appointing ministers, disclaiming them, and also excommunicating; but the last appeal is to the brethren of body of the church."[50] This statement referred to the congregation appointing pastors and ministers to preach, administer the sacraments, and to engage in church discipline under the authority of the congregation. The congregation became the final appeal in all matters of church polity.

In the year 1611, two years after Smyth's *Short Confession*, Helwys expanded upon the same issues in his "Declaration of Faith of English People Remaining in Amsterdam." Lumpkin states "the Confession shows considerable independence of thought and is rightly judged the first English Baptist Confession."[51] If Lumpkin is correct, then he has properly identified

---

46. Ibid., 66–67.

47. Estep, "Bold Architect," 26, states, "It may be assumed that Smyth's position here was representative of Helwys as well." Estep makes this argument in reference to Smyth's work, *The Character of the Beast*, referenced previously. This work represents Smyth's Baptist development of his personal ecclesiology. At this time, Helwys was a member of the Smyth congregation. He did follow the leadership and theology of his pastor. Therefore, a reasonable inference is that the general reference of Estep is applicable to all of Smyth's work during the same phase. That is the presupposition of this section.

48. Smyth, "Short Confession of Faith," 100–114.

49. The issue of infant baptism will be addressed in chapter 6.

50. Smyth, "Short Confession of Faith," 101.

51. Helwys, "Declaration of Faith," 115.

that Helwys took Smyth's articles and developed a more thorough Baptist ecclesiology. Helwys's comments on the church are listed in Articles 10–22.[52] He contributes twice the content on the church as compared to Smyth. Commenting on the role of pastors in Article 21, Helwys states:

> That these officers are to bee chosen when there are persons qual-ified according to the rules in Christs Testament, I. Tim. 3.2–7, Tit. 1.6–9. Act. 6.3.4. By election and approbacion off that Church or congregacion whereof they are members, Act. 6.3.4. and 14.23, with Fasting, Prayer, and Laying on off hands, Act. 13.3. and 14.23. And there being but one rule for Elders, therefore but one sort of Elders.[53]

In this article, Helwys addresses the role of pastors who are biblically quali-fied. He uses the same texts with which he addressed the Puritans in Book III of the *Mystery of Iniquity*. This indicates that he had developed his role of Baptist ecclesiological leadership prior to the return to England.

This article additionally reviewed the election of the pastor. Again, Helwys employed the same language in *Mystery of Iniquity* that is found in his "Declaration of Faith." In Article 21, he also rejects multiple elderships within leadership. He acknowledges the single-pastor rule, which is a rejec-tion of Presbyterianism, and the basic structure of English Separatism and the Church of England. The national church could have claims to the king being the head; however, Helwys made the claim that Baptist ecclesiology only recognized one king as the rightful head of the church, King Jesus.

Church Polity: Baptist Congregations
Under King Jesus' Headship

The rationale for the Puritans to remain in the national church was due partly to their allegiance to England. The king was a proclaimed Christian, which made it difficult for the Puritans to become Separatists. In other words, they not only had an allegiance to England, but to the crown as well.

Helwys accurately portrays the position of the Puritans as being more loyal to the King of England than to King Jesus. He presses the matter with a rhetorical question:

---

52. Ibid., 120–22.

53. Ibid., 122.

> We demand of you, how, if the king should be you to truly inform him whether it is more lawful for a Christian king to restrain the church of some of the ordinances which Christ has appointed than for a heathen king? It cannot be that you would tell the king that a Christian king might more lawfully do such evil than a heathen king . . . Why then, if a Christian king may not more lawfully do such evil, (as you hold it to be evil or else why cry out for much for reformation) neither may you more lawfully obey him in such than a heathen king.[54]

Helwys's argument is that the Puritans knew that they could not address the king in terms of him changing the law as to allow the church ordinances administered per Puritan reform. As a result, the Puritans were loyal to a king who was on a par with a pagan king.

In order to support his claim, Helwys used the biblical illustration of the apostles. He wrote:

> The disciples of Christ, who were more obedient subjects, taught you and us all obedience to our king. Yet they would not be restrained in the causes of God, but chose rather to obey God than men, and rather to suffer imprisonment and beating than to be restrained either preaching or practicing any of the ways of God. Although they were commanded, imprisoned, and beaten up by the high priest, the council, and all the elders of Israel that were not heathen governors, (Acts 5) those who were faithful disciples were content to obey in all sufferings. Such obedience you would have submitted to if your hearts had been upright to God and the king.[55]

Helwys used the apostles as an illustration of how a true subject of God is supposed to respond to earthly kings, governors, and authorities. He makes the point that a true disciple acknowledges the commands of God regardless of the king's command. The reason that the apostles could respond in such fashion is that their lives were committed to God in comparison to the Puritans whose lives were committed to the English king.

54. Helwys, *Mystery of Iniquity*, 229–30.

55. Ibid., 230.

Implications for Baptist Ecclesiology

The implication for Baptist ecclesiology is that a true church will only submit to the authority of Christ. Helwys continued to build the argument of Baptist ecclesiology as subject to only King Jesus when he stated:

> From this ground of truth we speak to you in the words of the Holy Ghost. He that has commanded in the church the true preaching of the word, true baptism, and true administration of the Lord's Supper, the same God has also commanded true government in the church . . . yet if you have a false government, you are transgressors of the whole law of God, and guilty of all.[56]

The point that Helwys made is that a Baptist church has a biblical foundation for its ministries, which fosters the preaching of the Word, administers the ordinances, and acknowledges that God commanded the church to embrace true government under the reign of King Jesus.

Helwys could advocate the government of the Baptist *ecclesia* on the basis that he developed it earlier in his "Declaration of Faith." Article 9, which is the first article out of the twelve articles that describe the church, addressed the role of Christ in relation to the church. Helwys stated:

> That IESUS CHRIST is Mediator off the New Testament between GOD and Man, 1 Tim. 2.5, having all power in Heaven and in Earth given vnto him. Mat. 28.18. Being the onely KING, Luke 1.33, PRIEST, Heb. 7.24, and PROPHET, Acts 3.22. Off his church, he also being the onely Law-giver, hath in his Testament set downe an absolute, and perfect rule off direction, for all persons, at all times, to bee observed; Which no Prince, nor anie whosever, may add to, or diminish from as they will avoid the fearful judgments denounced again them that shal so do. Revel. 22.18,19.[57]

Helwys had developed Baptist ecclesiology on the foundation that Christ is the only Head of the church. Therefore, he could inform the Puritans that they had made a mistake by acknowledging the temporal king as head of the Church of England. Submission to an earthly king could only have the logical force of replacing Jesus as king within any church government. Therefore, the reform the Puritans wanted was subject to King James I and not the Lord Jesus Christ.

---

56. Ibid., 236.

57. Helwys, "Declaration of Faith," 119.

One of the distinct hallmarks of Baptist ecclesiology is the fundamental truth for each Baptist congregation to embrace God's will without the interference of ecclesiastical authorities. Coupling this truth with the other biblical truth that only Jesus Christ governs the church means that each congregation submits to the rule of Christ in its ministries. Additionally, this truth was signified in the administering of the ordinances by the local church and not the national church. Thus, believer's baptism became the more accurate sign of the church instead of the national church's insistence on infant baptism. The argument against the Separatists revealed the depth of Helwys's heart for a true *ecclesia*, for instance, one that would perform the ministries of the Lord via the proclamation of the Word and the administering of the ordinances.

6

Helwys's Critique of Separatism

Introduction

IN BOOK IV OF *Mystery of Iniquity*, Helwys addresses the Separatist movement for their insistence on retaining infant baptism. Helwys states that "it is but the mere vain invention and tradition of men, which whoso follows can never have favor with God."[1] The issue of baptism for Helwys and the Separatists is not just a perceived ordinance holding little meaning. In fact, the ordinance of baptism revealed the depth of disagreement between the Separatists and the Baptists as the meaning is predicated upon the soteriology of the New Covenant.

In the last chapter, the issue of Puritanism and the Baptist reaction to their soteriology was the subject. The Puritans desired biblical reform, but sought it through magisterial means. Their goal was to retain a pure national church. The Separatists were much more radical in their theological conclusions. Separatism was founded on the theological principle that the Church of England could not be reformed and the only viable alternative was to leave.

This chapter will review English Separatism, Helwys's critique of the Separatist ecclesiological position, and the Separatist meaning of covenant. Then the chapter will progress in evaluating the rationale of Helwys's conclusion that Separatism was a deficient model of the New Covenant. The progression of the chapter will then examine John Smyth's theological

---

1. Helwys, *Mystery of Iniquity*, 120.

influence upon Thomas Helwys. The chapter will also review Baptist ecclesiology as a sufficient model of the New Covenant, Baptist Ecclesiology and Covenant, and will close with implications for Baptist ecclesiology.

Review of English Separatism

The English Separatist Movement started with strong discontent for Queen Mary's attempt to return England to Catholicism.[2] B. R. White claims that "the most significant of the various Protestant groups in England under Mary was undoubtedly that made up of those who may be fairly termed 'Edwardian Anglicans.'"[3] These Edwardian Anglicans were the forerunners to the Separatist movement. "Indeed, implicitly, and sometimes explicitly, the nonconforming Edwardian Anglicans under Mary became Separatists because they regarded the Roman Church and its ways as false and its worship as idolatrous."[4] The seeds of Separatism were in place, but the act of separating from the Church of England awaited two decades.

A definition of Separatism is valid in understanding the movement. The primary goal of establishing a New Testament church was at the core of Separatism. Thus, any definition must include the act of separation as well as the prescription of Separatism. James Leo Garrett gives a valuable definition of Separatists when attempting to discern the nature of the movement. "Separatists we understand to have been those English Puritans who, not being willing to continue to await thoroughgoing reforms in the Church of England, separated therefrom by constituting congregations or conventicles on the basis of a church covenant and congregational polity."[5]

The Separatist movement found theological ideology from the infamous writings of John Foxe. "On the whole, however, their prehistory was provided for them by John Foxe: from him both the Separatists and their more ecclesiological orthodox opponents were to draw most of their source material for reference to English martyrs and to Protestantism in England generally under Mary."[6]

---

2. The origin of Separatism was discussed in chapter 5. Therefore, a brief review will serve to refresh the reader of the basic tenets of the Separatist position.

3. White, *English Separatist Tradition*, 5.

4. Ibid., 6.

5. Garrett, *Four-Century Study*, 16.

6. White, *English Separatist Tradition*, 3.

In Foxe, the false church consistently persecuted the true church, thereby making reform impossible. This gave motivation for the Separatists to denounce the reform effort of the Puritans within the Church of England. The Separatists saw very little difference between English Roman Catholicism under Mary and the Settlement of Elizabeth. The idea to separate physically from that which is unholy is the culmination of attempting to reestablish New Testament Christianity.

A historical event demonstrating that Separatism had solidified as a theological concept prior to the advent of Robert Browne is recorded by Champlin Burrage. Separatists, either as an action of people or a specific reference to the movement, are mentioned in a letter from Bishop Grindal to Henry Bullinger, dated June 11, 1568.

> Some London citizens of the lowest order, together with four or five ministers, remarkable neither for their judgment nor learning, have openly *separated* from us [emphasis this writer's]; and sometimes in private houses, sometimes in the fields, and occasionally even in ships, they have held their meetings and administered sacraments.[7]

The letter references the "London citizens" separating from the Church of England. The contents of the paragraph suggest that the word "separated from us" may have been a descriptive term denoting the actions of the citizens in question. However, the term could also have been used in the vernacular of the day to allow Bishop Grindal not only to apply it to the actions, but also as a description of the people in question. Whether the actions of the London citizens can factually prove a separatist movement existed is debatable. Regardless of the specific meaning of Grindal, no question exists that the London citizens formed a congregation outside of the local parish.

Robert Browne emerged in the 1580s as a leader of the Separatists, but the movement itself was well-founded previous to his rise of leadership.[8] His leadership allows for the strong consideration that Separatism may have developed soon after the rise of Puritanism or perhaps even simultaneous to the Puritan movement.[9] If simultaneous, not much evidence

---

7. Burrage, *Early English Dissenters*, 80.

8. White, *English Separatist Tradition*, 44, is skeptical about Browne's involvement with the development of Separatism.

9. Griswold, "Congregational Dynamics," 64, states "the opinion of J. W. Marsden that it was the separated church of Richard Fitz that spawned those 'extreme Puritans'

exists to support the theory.[10] Regardless of the origins of the movement, a unifying theological position formed the Separatist identity, which moved away from the Puritans via a different understanding of the covenant.

Separatist Position on Covenant Ecclesiology

The basic difference between the Puritans and the Separatists was that Puritans remained in the Church of England, and the Separatists rejected the Church of England. The means for the differing actions is based upon their different understanding of the covenant. Puritans adhered to an unconditional covenant position, whereas Separatists came to the conclusion that the covenant was conditional.

Separatist/Puritan Meaning of Covenant

A brief review concerning the Puritan and Separatist historical theological concept of covenant is warranted. The Puritans via Marian exiles were exposed to Reformed Covenantal Theology. Basically the Old Testament Covenant, with an emphasis on the Abrahamic Covenant, was the foundational basis for God's soteriological work with humanity. The Old Covenant was logically extended to the New Covenant, which allowed the former to give the latter theological definition. This position is the legacy of John Calvin's teachings, "which were held in high esteem at the Oxford and Cambridge Universities."[11]

John Von Rohr describes the lineal process of the covenant through biblical examples.

---

who, in turn, spawned the Separatists that we recognize as the first Independent Congregationalist and Baptist." Griswold understands Marsden's position to be one of chronological order, i.e. first there were Puritans which, in turn, gave rise to the Separatists.

10. Ibid., 9–19. White builds a strong case for the existence of Separatism during the reign of Mary. The problem though is that the evidence he yields does not satisfy the question of categories. In other words, are not those meeting in the houses and not parishes to be considered as separatists in the sense that they denounced the national church, which was Romanish, or did they remain part of the Church of England (Rome) while meeting in conventicles? The fact is they were definitely congregations, but what was their relationship to the Church of England under the reign of Mary Tudor? Were they true separatists in the sense that they left the Church of England? White does not answer these questions.

11. Ibid., 33. See Calvin, *Institutes of the Christian Religion.*

That endeavor often bore close relationship to the idea of covenant, for in the federal theology of early Puritanism God entered into covenant commitments with men, and from beginning to end covenants encompassed and circumscribed the divine-human relationships. There had been the Covenant of Works with Adam. But after the fall of man God established his Covenant of Grace. This latter was itself distributed in several ways: promised in the Garden to fallen Adam, made more explicit in the dealings with Abraham, given added substance in the covenant of Sinai, and sealed and certified in the death of Christ, so that now men are incorporated under that New Covenant made most certain by him.[12]

The interpretative grid in Reformed Theology is basic to the Old and New Testaments. Every major soteriological event comes under the rubric that the event itself is related to God's covenant with Israel. Thus, *Heilsgeschichte* is the unfolding of God's covenant plan.

The continuity between the Old and New Testaments is seen in the relationship between the Old and New Covenants. Mark W. Karlberg stated:

One of the most complex topics in the whole of Christian doctrine, one particularly crucial for Reformed exegesis and theology, is the relationship between the Old and New Testaments, or to state the contrast . . . law of Moses and the law of Christ . . . Despite all the varieties of theological formulation held among the Puritans, however, there was underlying agreement concerning the nature and basis of salvation in Christ (specifically, the doctrine of justification by faith apart from the works of the law). The one way of salvation was applicable to the saints in all ages before and after Christ's coming. Likewise, there was unanimity concerning the binding character of the moral law for the believer (the normative regulative use of the law).[13]

The Puritan/Separatist understanding held the above in common. The theological continuity between both Testaments was foundational to their common understanding of God's redemptive plan. The basic meaning of covenant was a unilateral promise given unconditionally to God's elect. The elect were the recipients of the covenant and, therefore, no accord was given to humanity's ability to accept the covenant. The elect of the covenant received a gift from God, and as such, the gift of redemption was unconditional.

12. Von Rohr, "Covenant and Assurance in Early English Protestantism," 195.

13. Karlberg, "Moses and Christ," 13.

Separatist Divergence of Covenantal Meaning

The desire to form a church led the Separatists to embrace a different meaning of the covenant. Robert Browne began to realize that the English political system would not allow true reform to take place in the Church of England. Logically, the thought progressed upon the lines which acknowledged the national church as impure. Then the fault must be placed upon God who chose the elect to establish the church since the covenant was unconditional. This was an untenable position. Therefore, the meaning of covenant had to be reconsidered. Griswold stated:

> Impelled by their desire to form true, visible churches, constituted as companies of believers in covenant with God and each other, those Independents who separated from the Church to form gathered churches did so on the basis of a radically different interpretation of the meaning of "Covenant," one not of promise, but of a bilateral "contract" between two parties. Their version of the concept implied responsibility on the part of the saints to live lives of holiness, and to exercise the authority of the Lord to discipline its membership to keep the church pure by pressing apostates and offenders to repentance vis-à-vis the exercise of the "Keys of the Kingdom."[14]

The redefining of covenant allowed Browne the theological foundation to form a covenanted church.

Even though evidence of Separatism in the early 1560s exists, the movement that became known as Separatism did not become established until Robert Browne taught Separatist principles to Robert Harrison. Browne stated:

> Therefore both to R. H. & to the companie that aftervvard ioined, vvere such things spoken as follovve, & also set dove in Vvriting: namelie that vve are to forsake & denie all vngodlines & vvicked fellovveship, & to refuse all vngodlie communion vvith Vvicked persons. For this is it that is most & first of all needful: because God vvil receaue none to communion & couenant Vvith him, Vvhich as yet are at one vvith the Vvicked, or do openlie them selues transgresse his commaundementes.[15]

---

14. Griswold, "Congregational Dynamics," 34–35.

15. Browne, "True and Short Declaration," in *Writings*, 412.

Browne's writings reveal that he considered separating from the Church of England as the only viable option. The issue for consideration was that separation from the national church in order to form a local church would have been on the basis of reinterpretation of the covenant. Browne interpreted the covenant as entering into a relationship with God. The result was that the new interpretation was now conditional or bilateral.[16]

The impact of a bilateral covenant meant that the people of the congregation had the authority, under the headship of Christ, to form a congregation. The act of covenanting with one another effectively denied the authority of the state to impose their ecclesiology upon English citizens. The rationale for Browne's actions is that a true church would have the visible mark of holiness. Browne stated:

> The Church planted or gathered, is a companie or number of Christians or beleeuers, which by a willing couenant made with their God, are vnder the gouernment of god and Christ, and kepe his laws in one holie communion: because Christ hath redeemed them vnto holiness & happiness for euer, from which they were fallen by the sinne of Adam.[17]

The covenant, per Browne, meant that a Separatist church could enter into a voluntary agreement to live their lives in holiness to one another. Thus, the mark or characteristic of a true church is comprised of true Christians living accountable to each other under the Lordship of Jesus Christ. Jason Lee concurs as he stated, "A Christian's duty is to form a true church through covenanting with other believers to be faithful to God. The covenant then not only becomes central to church membership, but also is an essential mark of being a Christian."[18]

Browne's understanding of a conditional covenant enabled him to take the position that the Church of England had failed to stay in covenant relationship with God. This meant that Browne's congregation was taking a stand in contrast to the apocalyptic false church described so very well by John Foxe. Since the conditions of the covenant had not been met by the

---

16. Brachlow, *Communion of Saints*, 32–33, writes, "In Elizabethan England this conditional covenant motif—derived perhaps as much from the earlier Tudor protestantism of William Tyndale and others as it was through the forceful influence of the Rhineland theologians—came to full expression in the systematic works of puritan theologians such as Dudley Fenner and William Perkins."

17. Browne, "Book Which Sheweth the Life and Manners," in *Writings*, 253.

18. Lee, "Baptism and Covenant," 120.

national church, this dynamic allowed Browne to form a congregation that would focus upon covenant with God and with one another. White stated:

> As has already been suggested he saw the reformation of the Church fundamentally in Biblical terms: as the voluntary renewal of the covenant between God and his people after its conditions had been broken on the people's side by a period of apostasy. For him the true Christian community was a congregation which had covenanted together and with God to obey the divine law.[19]

For Browne, the covenant was not only a bilateral agreement with God and the church, but it was also to be interpreted as community that voluntarily covenanted together.

The new interpretation of the covenant now meant that Separatism held a distinct theological difference from the Puritans. The Puritans had adhered to the unconditional nature of the covenant, which meant that they would not leave the Church of England. In their minds, it was a true church that had flaws, which desperately needed reform. The Separatists, however, through the conditionality of the covenant, now possessed the theological foundation to leave the national church in order to reestablish a true visible church within England. "Thus, Robert Browne departed from the Puritan mainstream by carrying it to its logical conclusion of separation from the corruption and laxness he saw them willing to tolerate, seeing separation as the only way of dissociating from the ungodly."[20]

Old Covenant Continuity to New Covenant

No doubt exists that Browne's theology informed his ecclesiology. His ecclesiology demanded a pure, undefiled church. Again, apocalypticism helps place the era into perspective. Steve Brachlow stated, "Like Foxe, Elizabethan radical puritans believed that throughout the centuries the church had been caught in a cosmic conflict between light and darkness, Christ and Antichrist."[21] The Antichrist had entered the church through the Roman Papacy. The Elizabethan settlement still retained aspects of the Antichrist in the English church. The end result was that Parliament was content to work with Elizabeth, and the Puritans were content to stay a part

---

19. White, *English Separatist Tradition*, 54.
20. Griswold, "Congregation Dynamics," 69.
21. Brachlow, *Communion of Saints*, 79.

of the Church of England; therefore, the Separatists had little opportunity to reform the national church.

The Separatists did leave the Church of England to form independent congregations. The sign of the true church was retained in the lifestyle of the membership. Thus, covenant was the defining characteristic of a true church. Patrick Collinson stated:

> Such a situation pointed unmistakably to voluntarism and independency. In defending his non-separating position to separatists, William Ames proposed that the covenant by which an independent church is constituted had been made in effect by any group of Christians meeting together voluntarily. He might have added that some groups had gone so far as to formalize their meetings with a written covenant, subscribed by all the participants.[22]

The covenant being the focal point of separatism opens the question of the nature of the New Testament ordinances. What role did the ordinance of baptism have in a Separatist covenantal church?

The Separatists continued in the ecclesiological pattern of the Puritans. They understood baptism to be a seal of the covenant. Browne made the following statement concerning the nature of infant baptism with regard to the church.

> What is the covenant or condicion on our behalfe? We must offer and geue vp our selues to be of the church and people of God. We must likewise offer and geue vp our children and other vnder age, if they be of our householde and we haue full power ouer them. We must make profession, that we are his people, by submitting our selues to his laws and gouernement. How must Baptisme by vsed, as a seale of this covenaunt? They must de duelie presented, and offered to God, and the church, which are to be Baptised. They must be duelie receiued vnto grace and fellowship.[23]

Browne retained infant baptism as a sign or seal of the covenant made with God. The fact that he required parents to be Christians before they could offer their children to the church as members. The obligation of the parents was emphasized as it was their duty to offer the child for baptism. This allowed only those parents who offered themselves to the Lord and the Church to recommend their own children for baptism. Browne missed the issue on one vital point in that he did not address those who had received

22. Collinson, *Elizabethan Puritan Movement*, 381.

23. Browne, "Book Which Sheweth the Life and Manners," 256.

baptism by the Anglican Church or the Roman Church. He simply kept the reformed covenantal approach as the basis for his ecclesiology. Unfortunately, Browne never ventured to consider believer's baptism as being the proper subject of baptism. This was left to John Smyth and Thomas Helwys.

Separatist Ecclesiology as Deficient Model of New Covenant

The issue for Helwys was the meaning of baptism in relationship to ecclesiology. In Book IV, he condemns the Separatists for not being consistently biblical in the founding of their independent churches. He acknowledges the covenant foundation of Separatist churches. "And now to become Christ's you say you are called and separated from the world by the Word of God, and joined together by voluntary profession of the faith of Christ in the fellowship of the gospel. This is your confession, wherein you have erred, as may plainly appear."[24]

The error that Helwys spoke of concerns the relationship between baptism, the covenant, and church membership. He denounced that concept of a gathered community without the sign of entering that community, which was believer's baptism.

> And to show you that you are not joined to Christ, you being of the world before you constituted or set up your church by your own confessions, the Word of the Lord does evidently declare that there is no way for them that are of the world, who are not in Christ, but enemies to Christ, as all that are of the world are, there is no way to join and come to Christ, but only to "amend their lives, and be baptized" (Acts 2:38).[25]

Helwys made the point that a true church gives the testimony of baptism, which is the testimony of salvation. Therefore, a gathered community established by covenant was not the complete emergence of a New Testament Church.

24. Helwys, *Mystery of Iniquity*, 92.
25. Ibid.

Infant Baptism

Helwys does not fault the Separatists for covenanting together. He faults them for denying believer's baptism while they retain their infant baptismal practice. Using the apocalyptic language of the day, Helwys refers to the Separatists as false prophets, because they retained the baptism of Babylon, which is a reference to the Church of England.

> But your false prophets, to make good the retaining of your Baby-lonish baptism, like deep deceivers with turning of devices, plead that your baptism must be retained, and it not to be repeated, nor more that Israel's circumcision, when they came to the Passover in Hezekiah's time . . . But when you are called on for the retaining of your baptism you received in Babylon, then Israel's circumcision is your hold.[26]

A true church has the sign of baptism, which is based upon the confession and repentance of sin. When the Separatists were pressed to give an answer for their rationale in keeping infant baptismal practices, they retorted the reformed position of baptism being the sign of the New Covenant, as circumcision was the sign of the Old Covenant.

Separatists utilized the same interpretation that the Church of England had used, for example, Separatists, and not the whole nation, were in covenant relationship with God. The sign of the covenant was infant baptism, which in reality became a seal of the covenant. Daniel C. Lane stated, "Covenant theologians contend that circumcision (which was commanded to be given to infants) functioned as the seal of the covenant in the Old Testament, and that baptism replaced circumcision as the seal of the covenant in the New Testament."[27] Lane goes on to quote John Calvin for support. "Yet, if it enters anyone's mind to jest at infant baptism . . . he is mocking the command of circumcision given by the Lord."[28] The ecclesiological significance for Separatist churches means they understood infants to be already in covenant; therefore, they could take the seal of the covenant. Separatists understood that infants were part of the covenant by means of their parents presenting them to the church.[29]

---

26. Ibid., 95.

27. Lane, "Some Difficulties," 166.

28. Ibid. The exact quote is found in Calvin, *Institutes of the Christian Religion* 4.16.9.

29. Browne, "Book Which Sheweth the Life and Manners," 256.

The theological dynamic at work is revealing. The basis of separation was that the covenant should be interpreted as conditional. However, when the covenant was applied to infants via infant baptism, the Separatists changed their position and embraced the covenant as being unconditional. The Separatists were inconsistent in the interpretation of the covenant. They interpreted covenant as conditional upon their obedience to separate from the national church, but reverted back to the unconditional nature of the covenant when they were required to answer for their ecclesiological practices. Brachlow commented, "While Separatist propagandist invariably invoked a 'mutualist' covenant theology to justify separatism when confronting puritans and conformists, they now shifted ground and turned to the unconditional covenant concept when disputing with the new Baptists in their midst."[30]

Helwys recognized their appeal to conditionality of covenant when he stated their claim "that God never made a covenant with them."[31] He knew the Separatists had predicated their ecclesiology on the premise that it pleased God to reestablish the true church through separatist practices. The logical conclusion for the Separatists is the Church of England was no longer a biblical church. Yet, the Separatists insisted upon the validity of their baptism from the Church of England. Herein was the point Helwys used to argue that a Separatist church was not thoroughly reformed: if the Church of England was not a true church, how could the act of baptism be valid?

The logic Helwys employs is that a true church will administer proper baptism, which is believer's baptism. He argues this consistently in Book IV. For example, this lays the foundation for evangelizing the unbeliever. Building upon Mark 16:16, Helwys stated:

> Then you, being of the world, were infidels or unbelievers, and the Holy Ghost teaches that infidels or unbelievers must amend their lives and be baptized . . . And our Savior Christ, giving a general direction to his disciples to preach the Gospel to all, gives likewise a general direction what all unbelievers must do if they will be saved.[32]

---

30. Brachlow, *Communion of Saints*, 153.

31. Helwys, *Mystery of Iniquity*, 113. The Separatists were persuaded the Church of England had forfeited the covenant, which meant that God's covenant was no longer valid for England. Again, this was the conditional aspect of the covenant.

32. Ibid., 93.

Helwys denounced the Separatist movement for failure to understand the order of baptism. A profession of faith in Christ was the determining factor for anyone's baptism. Without such a profession, no change of the lifestyle occurs, and consequently no baptism should take place.

Helwys uses their unconditional interpretation of the covenant against them in the area of ecclesiology and baptism. "This straight are you now driven unto, either to confess that before your separation you were infidels or unbelievers, and then you must believe and be baptized, or else that you were believers and faithful, and have you separated from a faithful and believing people, and not from the world."[33] Helwys makes the point concerning the ecclesiology of the English national church: if they were a true church and the Separatists were converted and baptized in the Church of England, then their act of separating was invalid.

The call for the Separatists to return to the Church of England was illustrated by Robert Browne. Helwys noted the return of Browne to the Church of England.

> And you must return to your vomit with that false prophet, your first and chief shepherd, that has misled you upon these false grounds, who not being able (through his infidelity) to keep his face towards Jerusalem and the land of Canaan, has fainted in the way, and rebelled in the wilderness, and is returned to his so much formerly detested Babylon and Egypt.[34]

The reference to Robert Browne is the example Helwys used to make the case that if one's baptism is valid it had to be administered by a valid church. Whether or not Browne recognized this is not the issue. The act of returning to the church that administered the baptism was the issue. Helwys's point is that if the baptism is valid, the church must be valid. This point challenged the Separatists' position on their concept of valid infant baptismal practice.

Source of Infant Baptism

Helwys makes the case that England's baptism originated from Rome. By making this connection, he could associate the Separatists with the membership of England which, in turn, belonged to Rome.

33. Ibid.
34. Ibid.

> Therefore, Brownists must return to the Church of England, and
> the Church of England and the presbytery must return to Rome,
> and be all sheep of one sheepfold, and repent of your unjust sepa-
> ration from the body whereof you were, and are all members . . .
> You have and do all by one baptism put on Christ, and you all have
> brought that baptism from Rome.[35]

Per Helwys, the Separatists have not been thorough in their separation for the Church of England, which has not been thorough in its own reform. The origin of infant baptism that the Separatists insisted upon maintaining goes back to Rome.

Since the Separatists kept the practice of infant baptism, and if they justified their argument as valid, then no need existed for separation, making the apocalyptic-ecclesiological interpretation invalid. "Furthermore, if Rome be believers in Christ Jesus, then are these prophecies of scripture nowhere to be found fulfilled upon the whole earth."[36]

The point is obvious: why should the Separatists remove themselves from the membership of the Church of England, and why should the same church leave Rome if they have retained the covenantal seal of infant baptism as a biblical practice? The logic of Helwys's argument leads to the natural question of the necessity of reform.

> The Church of England and the presbytery do allow the baptizing
> of all the infants of Rome, . . . and the parents of the infants that are
> baptized, and those infants being already come to be men of years,
> would destroy the kings, and princes, and countries, and all them,
> *for professing Christ as they do* [emphasis this writer's].[37]

No need existed for any reform attempt if the Church of England and Roman Catholicism proclaimed Christ. This statement was the logical conclusion of the Separatists' desire to retain the practice of infant baptism.

Helwys is convinced that not only was infant baptism invalid, but the Separatists' interpretation of the covenant was erroneous. The Separatists' interpretation of the covenant was the core of the hermeneutical issue that allowed them to retain infant baptism. The interpretative issue is the exact point of difference between the Separatist movement and the Baptist movement.

35. Ibid., 115.
36. Ibid.
37. Ibid., 119.

John Smyth's Influence Upon Thomas Helwys

Smyth was Thomas Helwys's pastor until the former decided to make church membership application to the Mennonites. His influence upon Thomas Helwys has been the subject of much thought.[38] By the time of the 1606 Coventry Conference, Smyth and Helwys had been friends for a year. After their attempts at Hampton Court were not as successful as hoped, the conference was a meeting of Puritan clergy for the purpose of discussing their options.[39] Jeong In Choi depicts that Smyth and Helwys became Separatists together after they attended the Coventry Conference in 1606.

> Smyth expressed his belief to his Puritan friends that his only choice was to leave the Church of England and become a Separatist. Helwys likewise demonstrated firm resolve to move from Puritanism to Separatism. Thus Smyth and Helwys joined the ranks of the Separatists together, officially separating from the Church of England shortly after the conference.[40]

The fact that both men were Separatists meant they had embraced the concept of a covenanted and gathered church. Separatist ecclesiological principles were embedded in their minds and flowed outwardly in their actions.

Baptist Pastor and Baptist Layman[41]

Smyth led the Gainsborough Church to Amsterdam where the members escaped persecution for their Separatist position. McBeth stated, "Apparently Helwys was a leader, for one record says that if Smyth 'brought oares, Helwys brought sayles.' . . . If Smyth was the more dynamic and creative, Helwys made his contribution in clarity of thought and stability of action."[42]

Smyth debated with other Separatist churches in Amsterdam, most notably Francis Johnson and the Ancient Church. "This conflict led Smyth to publish *The Difference of the Churches*, which he describes as 'a correction

---

38. For an exhaustive review of the Smyth/Helwys relationship, see Choi, "Relationship of John Smyth and Thomas Helwys."

39. White, *English Separatist Tradition*, 121–22.

40. Choi, "Relationship of John Smyth and Thomas Helwys," 69.

41. For a more comprehensive historical review, please see chapter 1.

42. McBeth, *Baptist Heritage*, 34.

and svpplement' to Principles and Inferences."[43] This debate in 1608 served as the catalyst for Smyth "to question the validity of Separatist churches."[44]

The Character of the Beast.[45] Smyth's debate with Richard Clyfton was chronicled in the work, *The Character of the Beast.*

> This dispute started after Smyth had become convinced of the error of infant baptism. White comments that Smyth came to the conclusion that infant Baptist was heretical because of three issues within Separatism's background. First, there was a longstanding unease of most Separatists with the baptism which they had received in what they believed to be the apostate Church of England. Secondly, there was the continuing Bible study which stemmed from their restless desire to re-model the visible church ever more closely towards what they believed to be the apostolic ideal. Thirdly, there was the practice of believer's baptism by the Mennonites in Amsterdam. Their unease must have sharpened the question, their Bible study and their knowledge of Mennonite practice may well have provided an answer.[46]

Regardless of how Smyth came to his conclusion, he did reject infant baptism as a seal of the covenant.

Even though he rejected infant baptism, he never rejected the covenanted community concept of a New Testament Church. In his work, *Parallels and Inferences*, Smyth wrote, "The outward part of the true forme of the true visible church is a vowe, promise, oath, or covenant betwixt God and the Saints . . . This covenant hath 2 parts. 1. Respecting God and the faithful. 2. Respecting the faithful mutually." [47]

The issue for Smyth was the question of a biblical sign of the Covenant. He rejected infant baptism, because it was not a sign of the covenant. The new birth convinced him that the sign or seal of God's covenant relationship with his people was the Holy Spirit. He stated:

> There are two seales: Circumcision a seale of the carnal covenant vppon the carnal children: Gen. 17.11 & the Holy Spirit of promise a seale of the Spirituall covenant vppon the Spirituall seed . . . Gen. 17.10.11.12. this place proveth that circumcision was a seale of the

---

43. Lee, *Theology of John Smyth*, 52.

44. Choi, "Relationship of John Smyth and Thomas Helwys," 101.

45. Smyth, *Character of the Beast*, in Works, 2:563–680.

46. White, *English Baptists of the Seventeenth Century*, 19.

47. Smyth, *Principles and Inferences*, in Works, 1:254.

> carnall covenant made with the carnall seed, & not a seale of the
> Spirituall covenant made with the Faithful: For the Spirit is the seale
> thereof, who is therefor called the Spirit of promise, & the seale.[48]

Acknowledging the Holy Spirit as the means of entry into the New Covenant forced a decisive break with Separatism.

Separatism had based its church on the practice of a conditional covenant, which meant that they also embraced infant baptism. They did not seek a new baptism, as the sign of the covenant meant that the church member parent could present the child as a covenant member. Smyth attacked the Separatists for not being consistent in their approach to ecclesiology. Smyth declared, "Infants are not actuall beleevers . . . so infants are not vnder the everlasting covenant of Abraham."[49] The rationale for Smyth was that the infants could not believe in Christ as they were incapable of making a profession of faith by repenting of sin. Thus, the visible sign of the church could not be infant baptism, but rather had to be the evidence of the Holy Spirit at work in the life of a true believer. James Coggins states:

> In arguing for believers' baptism he emphasized the superiority
> of the spiritual New Testament covenant to the carnal Old Testament covenant, the spiritual seal of circumcision of the heart to
> carnal seals like physical circumcision and baptism, and the spiritual second birth to physical birth as a prerequisite for entrance
> into the covenant.[50]

The emphasis on the Holy Spirit, and particularly the new birth, as visible signs of the new covenant meant that Smyth had become a Baptist in 1608, and Helwys followed his pastor's leadership.

Helwys's Commitment to Baptist Ecclesiology

Helwys was the faithful layman and supporter of John Smyth. W. T. Whitley comments, "Thomas Helwys, evidently about the same age as Smyth, soon became his closest friend."[51] The friendship between the two men evolved into a mentorship. However, Helwys was committed to Baptist principles more so than he was to Smyth. Once Helwys had learned the distinctive ar-

---

48. Smyth, *Character of the Beast*, 2:580–81.

49. Ibid., 2:607.

50. Coggins, "Theological Positions of John Smyth," 256.

51. Whitley, "Biography," lvi.

guments for Baptist ecclesiology, he would not leave them to follow Smyth. In fact, the ecclesiology he learned from Smyth was basically the same arguments Smyth used in his writings.

Comparison Between Smyth and Helwys

The similarities between Helwys's *Mystery of Iniquity* and Smyth's *The Character of the Beast* reveal the depth to which Helwys was committed to Baptist ecclesiology. Three items for comparisons, which reveal this commitment are the use and interpretation of covenant, the seal of the Holy Spirit and his relationship to baptism, and Helwys's usage of Smyth's argumentation against Richard Clyfton.

The first area to consider is the following interpretation of covenant from the accounts of Smyth and Helwys. Smyth stated:

> One covenant was made with Abraham & his carnal seed & of that covenant was circumcision a seale: another covenant made with Abrha & his Spiritual seed, & of that covenant the holy Spirit of promise is the seale: for the carnal covenant had a carnal seale vppon the carnal seed: the Spiritual covenant had a Spiritual seale vppon the Spiritual seed.[52]

Smyth continues on to say:

> Baptisme is not the seale of the old Test, & that infants of the old Testa. Were capable of circumcision absolutely seeing that to be circumcised ther was nothing required but a forskinne apt to be cut of: but to baptism in the new Test. ther is required actual faith & repentance confessed by the mouth, Mat. 3.6. Act. 4.37 &10.47.[53]

Smyth's argument denies the continuity between the Old and New Covenants. He based this on the Old Covenant's carnal nature.[54] The sign of the Old Covenant was external via circumcision. This sign did not require faith and repentance; thus, Smyth deemed it carnal. The sign of the New Covenant is baptism, which does require faith and repentance. Per Smyth, no continuity exists between the signs of the Old and New Covenants.

Helwys utilized the same argument and nearly the same language against the Separatists.

52. Smyth, *Character of the Beast*, 2:579–80.

53. Ibid., 2:593.

54. Ibid., 2:579.

> But if you will have infants baptized, that is, washed with water and certain words, then you bring in a carnal rite, which purges not the conscience (for you do not hold that the infants' conscience are purged thereby), and so do you make the new covenant and ordinances carnal, like unto the old, which may not be, except you will directly oppose the evident Word of the Lord, as you have long herein done, to your utter destruction, except you repent.[55]

Helwys interpreted the Old Covenant as having a carnal nature. The New Covenant was spiritual as evidenced by his comparison of the New Covenant to the carnality of the old one.

The New Covenant is for the New Testament church; therefore, Helwys will not revert back to a Separatist position. The argument against the Separatists' infant baptism is made on the basis of the Old Covenant being established for its own purpose. Like Smyth, Helwys rejected any continuity of the Old Covenant sign of circumcision and the New Covenant sign of baptism.

> And all this is most plainly set down in that Epistle to the Hebrews, which differences between the old and new covenant, if it were carefully searched unto and found out, it would overthrow your deceitful consequence which you draw from covenants that are dislike, or not like in substance, contrary to all understanding. And it would make you cast away your carnal baptizing of infants and to baptize no infants.[56]

Helwys viewed the Old Covenant in terms of carnal and as being very different from the spiritual New Covenant. They were not the same in substance. The comparison between Smyth and Helwys revealed that Helwys retained the argumentation Smyth taught him, which allowed both men to formulate their positions on Baptist ecclesiology. In other words, Helwys did not abandon Smyth's interpretive scheme.

The second issue for consideration is the phrases Smyth and Helwys used when describing the seal of the Holy Spirit in relation to baptism. Smyth stated:

> I desire to be enformed in al the Scriptures where baptisme is called a seale of the new Testament, though I cannot deny that the baptisme of the holy ghost is the seale. I say thereof that the seale of the Spirit must go befor the baptisme of water: & as al the

55. Helwys, *Mystery of Iniquity*, 123.
56. Ibid., 125.

ordinances of the new Testament are Spritual, & yet visible, so is
the seale of the new Testament Spiritual, & yet visble.[57]

Smyth denies the act of water baptism as a seal of the covenant. He places
the act of sealing the New Testament Covenant with salvation and the seal
of the Holy Spirit. By doing so, baptism becomes a sign of the seal and not
the seal itself.

Helwys uses the same argument, and again, nearly the same language
as he challenges the Separatists on the meaning of the seal.

> If you will examine the New Testament throughout, you shall find
> no seal, nor none sealed, but they that believe, "who are sealed
> with the Holy Spirit of Promise." . . . The Seal of the covenant
> must needs be answerable to that holy covenant, a seal of life and
> salvation only to them that believe and are baptized. (Ephesians
> 1:13–14; Revelation 2:17–18) The apostle here to the Ephesians
> does show that "after they believed they were sealed with the Holy
> Spirit of promise."[58]

The concept both men attempted to prove is the New Testament does not
have an outward seal of the covenant. It has the inward seal of the Holy
Spirit, and the outward sign of baptism demonstrates the inward seal. This
line of reasoning serves to demonstrate the lack of continuity between the
Old and New Covenants. It also yields the conclusion that infants should
not be baptized, as there is not an outward sign to give them, because they
do not qualify via repentance for the inward seal of the Holy Spirit.

The final issue for comparison is the argumentation used against
Richard Clyfton. Smyth answered the argument Clyfton proposed for the
Separatists to retain their own infant baptism. Smyth restated Clyfton's
argument:

> As the Babilonians abuse of the vessels of the L. howse did not
> make a nullity of them, but were vsed after the captivity, Ezra. 1.11.
> so the Antichristian abuse of baptisme cannot disannul it, but it
> may bee retained when men come to the Fayth: & it needeth not
> to be reiterated, no more then the vessels of the howse of the Lord
> be new cast.[59]

---

57. Smyth, *Character of the Beast*, 2:586.
58. Helwys, *Mystery of Iniquity*, 127–28.
59. Smyth, *Character of the Beast*, 2:647.

Clyfton argued that the vessels of the Babylonian captivity were reused without being made anew. This was his reply to Smyth for keeping the infant baptism of England and not baptizing each member anew. Clyfton was persuaded that, even though the Church of England was apostate, their infant baptism was still valid. Smyth continues on to say:

> I answer many things: First this arg. is an excellent arg. for the retaining of idoll Temples, the worship, government, ministery of the ecclesiastical assemblies of England: if it be said they were never appointed by God, so say I, that baptisme of theirs was never appointed by God: but is the devise of Antichrist. Secondly, I answer, that the vessels of the Lords howse were his owne ordināces, & therfor need not to be new cast: But the baptism of Antichr. is not the L. owne ordinance . . . That baptisme is Antichr. invention in the definition of it.[60]

In a somewhat comical to sarcastic tone, Smyth answered Clyfton that infant baptism was idol worship created by the Antichrist and not of the Lord. Thus, should the Separatists keep their infant baptism, they are not following true reform and do not have a true church constitution.

Once again, Helwys utilized the same language and argumentation from Smyth. The difference is that Helwys is addressing John Robinson. Helwys stated:

> You say, "Baptism is the vessel of the Lord, and as when the house of the Lord was destroyed, and the vessels thereof, together with the people were carried into Babylon, they remained still the vessels of the Lord's house in nature, and right, though profaned by Belshazzar and made quaffing bowls, and being brought again out of Babylon to the house of the Lord were not to be new cast, (being purified) might again be used to holy use. So this vessel baptism though profaned in Babylon being brought again to the house of the Lord, remains still the holy vessel of the Lord."[61]

Helwys goes on to state:

> The vessels of the Lord are brought again to the house of the Lord, and are sanctified, but Belshazzar's drinkings in them and profaning of them is cast away as abominable . . . And thus must your baptizing be cast away and may not be permitted in the house of the Lord, . . . by this example to being in an imagination, as though

60. Ibid., 2:648.

61. Helwys, *Mystery of Iniquity*, 106.

> your baptism were brought out of the house of the Lord, when it is brought forth of the assemblies of England, with whom you justify God never made a covenant and they were never his people, nor God their God.[62]

Helwys uses Smyth, but expands upon his argumentation to make the connection that since the Separatists deemed the Church of England as apostate and not a covenantal people, their own personal baptism also is derived from the apostate. The conclusion is that logically, if the act of baptism had been defiled, it must be recovered from that which is fallen.

A summary of the Smyth-Helwys comparisons are in order. The comparisons that were analyzed reveal the ecclesiological debt of Helwys to Smyth, for example, the Gainsborough pastor taught the layman quite well. Yet, the comparisons of Smyth and Helwys also reveal the depth to which Helwys believed that Smyth had led him and others to recover the New Testament pattern of the church. Helwys used Smyth's arguments in much the same way Smyth did. The one difference, though, is that Helwys's ecclesiological convictions compelled him to stay with Baptist ecclesiology without the thought of returning to Separatism or venturing toward Anabaptism.

Baptist Ecclesiology as a Consistent Model of the New Covenant

Helwys maintained the position that believer's baptism was the identifying characteristic of a New Testament church. His position was predicated upon a different understanding of the covenant. Helwys maintained the Separatist tradition that covenant and ecclesiology were interwoven. His different interpretation of the covenant rested upon the fact that grace was to be proclaimed to all of humanity. "The Lord on his behalf does covenant that he will put and write his law in men's hearts by the power of his Spirit in the preaching of the Gospel, and he will be their God and save them."[63]

This does not mean that Separatists would disagree with Helwys. They would also proclaim the Gospel. The difference though is that Helwys was persuaded that the Gospel must be proclaimed before the ordinance of baptism could be administered. Thus, he logically questioned the Separatist

---

62. Ibid., 108.
63. Ibid., 121.

meaning of the covenant. "And first, we pray all those whose hearts God has inclined to seek his truth, and who desire in uprightness to walk in the light, that they will duly consider what the covenant of the Gospel is, and with whom it is made."[64]

Helwys does not interpret the covenant to be between God and the Separatists. He understands the covenant centers upon the Gospel. He interprets Jeremiah 31:33 and Hebrews 8:10 as God's desire to redeem people so that they will be the people of God. Helwys understands Mark 16:16, as Jesus' mission was to proclaim the Gospel to every person. Using these passages as his theological basis allow him to embrace a systematic approach to the covenant.

After the Gospel proclamation, the response to the Gospel is a personal belief in the message and the person is subsequently baptized. Helwys's argument is the Gospel does not allow infant baptism as an infant cannot respond. He goes on to make the point that the parents of an infant are not commanded to baptize their children. "Let them, we say, search, examine, and try by what show of truth it can possibly be conceived that under, or by this covenant of the new testament infants should be baptized, where the Lord requires no such things in this covenant of men to baptize their infants"[65] The result of the argument is that infants are not part of the New Testament church. Helwys effectively denied infant baptism as a sign or seal of the covenant.

The means of entering the covenant is salvation. If baptism is not a seal, but rather serves as a sign to the seal, the sign must point to the inward reality of the covenantal promise that God would create a new heart for his people. Helwys stated:

> But it is covenant in the Spirit, a spiritual covenant written in the hearts and minds of God's people, established upon better promises than the first covenant. And all this is evident by the words of the covenant, which are, "They that believe and are baptized shall be saved." And as this covenant is spiritual, so is the priesthood, so is the tabernacle, and all the ordinances, sacrifices, and services thereof.[66]

The covenant was nothing less than a relationship with the maker of the covenant, the Triune God.

64. Ibid.
65. Ibid.
66. Ibid., 125.

Baptist Ecclesiology and the Covenant

The concept of covenant and believer's baptism are where Separatists and Baptists parted as a group. Baptists, like Separatists, embraced the ecclesiological concept of a gathered covenanted community. Helwys understood covenant to mean it contained both vertical and horizontal relationships. He stated:

> Here is the new covenant set down by the Holy Ghost, both on God's behalf, and on their behalf with whom it is made, . . . The Lord on *his behalf* [emphasis this writer's] does covenant that he will put and write his law in men's hearts by the power of his Spirit in the preaching of the Gospel, and he will be their God and save them. And the covenant on *his people's behalf* [emphasis this writer's] which they are to keep and perform is to believe the Gospel and be baptized.[67]

Helwys did not challenge the unconditional nature of the covenant. The Lord covenanted himself to save his people, which reveals the unconditional nature of the covenant. Helwys understood the conditional aspect of the covenant as binding upon the people to relate to God and one another.

Divine and Human Relationships in the Covenant

Helwys was Trinitarian in thought. He revealed the Holy Spirit as God who convicts the person to be saved and then subsequently seals that person in redemption. The fact that Jesus Christ secured the atonement for a person to be saved is evidenced when Helwys stated, "Then shall men learn to know the true baptism of Christ, which is the 'baptism of repentance for remission of sins,' and be therewith baptized and 'put on Christ.'"[68] The plan of salvation is the culmination of the Father's promise to redeem his people.

Eternal Covenant

The eternal covenant is God's promise to redeem humanity. The inner life of the Trinity is extended to the individual conditional upon his/her

67. Ibid., 121.
68. Ibid., 147.

salvation.[69] The issue to grasp is the inner divine life of the Trinity extending relationship to humanity by means of the Gospel proclamation. Upon responding to the proclamation, humanity enters into Trinitarian life by means of salvation. The aspect of eternal life must be given to humans by the Holy Spirit through the sacrifice of the Son. Thus, Helwys could write that "God on his behalf does covenant that he will put and write his law in men's hearts by the power of his Spirit in the preaching of the Gospel."[70] This act of salvation is God's covenanted obligation to save humans upon their repentance of sin and belief in the Savior.

Local Covenant

The local covenant is the gathering of the people of God to live together in faithfulness to the Lord. The idea of "gathering and covenanted" is directly related to Matthew 18:20, which states that where two or three gather in the name of Christ, He is among them. The underlying meaning is that no gathering will occur unless they have responded to the Gospel message. The idea of gathering means that the Gospel has been proclaimed and responded to with favor. Helwys propagated this concept when he wrote, "And the covenant on his people's behalf which they are to keep and perform is to believe the Gospel and be baptized."[71]

Helwys articulated Smyth's ecclesiology. The assumption can be made that Helwys follows Smyth concerning the nature of the gathered church. Paraphrasing Smyth Paul S. Fiddes stated, "he evidently intends his treatise on the nature of the church to be a working out of the 'ordinances of Christ for the dispensing of the covenant since his death' and this is the eternal covenant of grace."[72]

---

69. Fiddes, *Tracks and Traces*, 26. Fiddes explains Calvinism developed the concept of a divine transaction between the Father and Son, which eventually culminated into the Westminster Confession. The theological concept of divine transaction denied any possibility that the eternal covenant could be conditional. The intended meaning of the book does not allow for decrees, but does allow for the eternal nature of soteriology as conditioned upon response by humanity, for instance, the confession of sin and belief in the death, burial, and resurrection of Jesus Christ.

70. Ibid., 121.

71. Ibid.

72. Fiddes, *Tracks and Traces*, 33.

Local Expression of the Eternal Covenant

Helwys's rejection of the Separatists was based upon his insistence that Separatism did not form a true church. By retaining infant baptism, Helwys did not think that the expression of the covenant in the local church was by means of infant baptism. Like Smyth, he connected the eternal covenant in the local church by means of Gospel proclamation and subsequent believer's baptism. Only believers could demonstrate the sign of the covenant of grace, for instance, water baptism after the inward spiritual baptism.

For one to enter the eternal covenant by means of the local gathered church, salvation was the prerequisite. In effect, this had the ability to safeguard the life of the church, if for no other reason, all members made a profession of faith. The nature of a local church that covenants together means that as a person enters the local covenant of believers, they are congruently entering the eternal covenant of grace. Fiddes states, "God the Father makes covenant of love eternally with the Son in the fellowship of the Spirit, so simultaneously God makes covenant in history with human beings."[73]

Implications for Baptist Ecclesiology

Helwys revealed that the implications for Baptist ecclesiology require a proper understanding of the ordinance of baptism. The focus on baptism itself is not only unwarranted, but also theologically incorrect. Baptism can only be correctly understood in relation to the gathered community of believers. The church has the covenant obligation to proclaim the Gospel and baptize those who respond; thus, infants are not to be baptized as they are not members of the gathered church. An infant cannot confess sin, which in turn leads one to make a profession of faith.

A second implication for Baptist ecclesiology is the covenant itself. When believers join together in covenanted churches, they have entered the inner life of the Trinity corporately. The Godhead is the source of eternal life for the individual believer and the source of life and headship for the church. The logical implication of this should be obvious; however, in order to be clear, no earthly ecclesiastical authority exists within or without the church. The pastor, individual officers, and members serve the Lord and one another under the Lordship of Christ in his church.

73. Ibid., 36.

Helwys underscored a sensitive point for Baptist ecclesiology. A church cannot alter the mode or subject of baptism and hope to maintain a healthy church. Since the ordinance of water baptism reflects the inward baptism of the Holy Spirit, the church can ill afford the loss of meaning by baptizing one who has made no profession of faith. Baptism is not a prerequisite to salvation, but rather a testimony of faith. Helwys's words for a gathered community, which did baptize without a proper profession of faith, were harsh but effective: he said they "had a false profession, and a false Christ."[74] The point is that Christ would not baptize a person unless a profession of faith was proclaimed. Helwys doubts that Christ could be a part of the church that embraces such heresy.

Another implication of Helwys's thought for Baptist ecclesiology is that the covenant demands discipline. Jason Lee states "To enter the public body of the church, the covenant offered by God must be agreed upon by the individual. The individual makes his consent visible to fellow believers through the sign of baptism. Baptism fulfills the role of agreeing to the local church covenant."[75] This approach allows one who is baptized to identify with Christ and with the body of Christ. Therefore, should a member not live according to the covenant, the member is subject to the discipline of the body as unto the Lord.

The final implication for Baptist ecclesiology is the focus upon proclamation. The gathered church covenanting together, living out the visible signs of the ordinance, allows the church to proclaim the Gospel to the world. Helwys demonstrated the conditional nature of the covenant. The condition is the response of the people to the Gospel proclamation. The church must realize that the primary task is the Gospel presentation to the world.

The Gospel proclamation is the very reason that Helwys returned to England. People in the Baptist church in Amsterdam did not have the ability to speak the Dutch language. Helwys knew that a return to England would in likelihood bring persecution to him and the congregation. Regardless of the probable scenario, he found precedent for that very issue in the Scriptures. Citing Paul in 1 Thessalonians 2:14, Helwys interpreted Paul to have stated that the church suffered persecution because of the Gospel. "Thus does the apostle commend to the churches of Judea, and of Thessalonica, for their constant suffering of persecution in their countries,

74. Helwys, *Mystery of Iniquity*, 92.
75. Lee, "Baptism and Covenant," 135.

not once advising them to fell out of their countries to avoid persecution. This is a new doctrine of devils brought in by men, that were found in the faith."[76] Helwys arrived at the conclusion that the Gospel is the means of eternal life, and the church had a mandate to proclaim the message regardless of the personal cost.

The purpose of the book was to examine Thomas Helwys's work, *A Short Declaration of the Mystery of Iniquity*, in order to determine its importance as a seminal contribution to Baptist ecclesiology. The main issue of research focused upon Helwys's thesis, which revealed Baptist ecclesiology as the only true church. The data surveyed was the content of *A Short Declaration of the Mystery of Iniquity*, the historical context of the writing, and the relevant themes he deemed appropriate. The theological content of the Church of England, the Puritans, and the Separatists were examined and compared to the arguments that Helwys set forth in order to establish Baptist ecclesiology.

Helwys attempted to establish a truly reformed *ecclesia* that was governed by the biblical and ecclesiological revelation. Personal conviction allowed Helwys to demonstrate the deficiency of the Church of England, Puritanism, and Separatism. The data revealed Helwys did expound upon Baptist ecclesiology as sufficient against the previous mentioned ecclesiologies. Helwys concluded that even though the various ecclesiologies should be free to practice their forms of church, they were, nonetheless, insufficient per the biblical model. According to Helwys, the true reformed church is a Baptist *ecclesia*.

76. Helwys, *Mystery of Iniquity*, 151.

Bibliography

Augustine. *The City of God*. Translated by Marcus Dods under the title *St. Augustine's The City of God*. In *NPNF*, series 2, edited by Philip Schaff, 2:1–511. American ed. Peabody, MA: Hendrickson, 1994.

———. *On Baptism, against the Donatists*. Translated by J. R. King. In *NPNF*, series 2, edited by Philip Schaff, 4:411–514. American ed. Peabody, MA: Hendrickson, 1994.

Bale, John. *The Image of Both Churches*. In *Select Works of John Bale: Containing the Examinations of Lord Cobham, William Thorpe, and Anne Askewe, and The Image of Both Churches*, edited by Henry Christmas, 249–640. Parker Society 1. Cambridge: Cambridge University Press, 1849.

Bauckham, Richard. *Tudor Apocalypse: Sixteenth Century Apocalypticism, Millennarianism, and the English Reformation: From John Bale to John Foxe and Thomas Brightman*. Oxford: Courtenay, 1978.

Bender, Harold Stauffer. "John Smyth and the Dutch Mennonites—A Communication." *Mennonite Quarterly Review* 4 (1930) 306–7.

Brachlow, Stephen. *The Communion of Saints*. Oxford: Oxford University Press, 1988.

———. "More Light on John Robinson and the Separatist Tradition." *Fides et Historia* 13 (1980) 6–22.

———. "Puritan Theology and General Baptist Origins." *Baptist Quarterly* 31 (1985) 179–94.

Brauer, Jerald C. "The Nature of English Puritanism: Reflections on the Nature of English Puritanism." *Church History* 23 (1954) 99–108.

Browne, Robert. "A Book Which Sheweth the Life and Manners." In *The Writings of Robert Harrison and Robert Browne*, edited by Albert Peel and Leland H. Carlson, 221–395. London: Routledge, 2003.

———. "A True and Short Declaration." In *The Writings of Robert Harrison and Robert Browne*, edited by Albert Peel and Leland H. Carlson, 396–429. London: Allen & Unwin, 2003.

Burgess, Walter H. *John Smith the Se-Baptist, Thomas Helwys and the First Baptist Church in England: With Fresh Light Upon the Pilgrim Fathers' Church*. London: Clarke, 1911.

Burrage, Champlin. *The Early English Dissenters in the Light of Recent Research (1550–1641)*. 2 vols. New York: Russell & Russell, 1966.

Bibliography

Calvin, John. *Institutes of the Christian Religion*. Edited by John T. McNeill. Translated by Ford Lewis Battles. Library of Christian Classics 20–21. Philadelphia: Westminster, 1960.

Canipe, Lee. "'That Most Damnable Heresie': John Smyth, Thomas Helwys, and Baptist Ideas of Freedom." *Baptist Quarterly* 40 (2004) 389–411.

Cathcart, William. *The Baptist Encyclopedia Baptist*. Baptist History Collection. Version 1 [CD-ROM]. Paris, AR: Baptist Standard Bearer, 2005.

Chibi, Andrew A. "Richard Sampson, His 'Oratio' and Henry VIII's Royal Supremacy." *Journal of Church and State* 39 (1997) 543–60.

Choi, Jeong In. "The Relationship of John Smyth and Thomas Helwys and its Impact on the Emergence of English General Baptists." PhD diss., New Orleans Baptist Theological Seminary, 2001.

Christian, John T. *A History of the Baptists: Together with Some Account of Their Principles and Practices*. Nashville: Broadman, 1922.

Christiansen, Paul. *Reformers and Babylon*. Toronto: University of Toronto Press, 1978.

Clark, Henry W. *A History of English Nonconformity: From Wiclif to the Close of the Nineteenth Century*. London: Chapman and Hall, 1911.

Clayton, J. Glenwood. "Thomas Helwys: A Baptist Founding Father." *Baptist History and Heritage* 8 (1973) 2–15.

Coggins, James R. *John Smyth's Congregation: English Separatism, Mennonite Influence, and the Elect Nation*. Studies in Anabaptist and Mennonite History. Scottdale, PA: Herald, 1991.

———. "The Theological Positions of John Smyth." *Baptist Quarterly* 30 (1984) 247–64.

Coker, Joe L. "Cast Out from Among the Saints: Church Discipline Among Anabaptists and English Separatists in Holland, 1590–1620." *Reformation* 11 (2006) 1–27.

Collins, Jeffery R. "The Restoration Bishops and the Royal Supremacy." *Church History* 68 (1999) 549–80.

Collinson, Patrick. "Antipuritanism." In *The Cambridge Companion to Puritanism*, edited by John Coffey and Paul C. H. Lim, 19–33. Cambridge: Cambridge University Press, 2008.

———. *The Elizabethan Puritan Movement*. Oxford: Oxford University Press, 1990.

Conrad, Russell. "Parliament, the Royal Supremacy and the Church." *Parliamentary History* 19 (2000) 27–37.

Cross, F. L., and E. A. Livingston, eds. *Oxford Dictionary of the Christian Church*. 3rd ed. Oxford: Oxford University Press, 1997.

Crumrine, Harrison. "The Oxford Martyrs and the English Protestant Movement, 1553–58." *Historian* 70 (2008) 75–90.

Culpepper, Scott. *Francis Johnson and the English Separatists Influence*. Macon, GA: Mercer University Press, 2011.

Deibler, Edwin C. "Chief Characteristics of Early English Puritanism." *Bibliotheca Sacra* 129 (1972) 326–36.

Deweese, Charles, W. *Baptist Church Covenants*. Nashville: Broadman, 1990.

Dickens, A.G. *The English Reformation*. New York: Schocken, 1964.

Durnbaugh, Donald F. "Free Churches, Baptists, and Ecumenism: Origins and Implications." *Journal of Ecumenical Studies* 17 (1980) 3–20.

Early, Joe Jr. "The Apocalyptic Nature of Thomas Helwys's Writings." In *American Baptist Quarterly* 28 (2009) 457–58.

Elton, G. R. *The Tudor Constitution: Documents & Commentary*. Cambridge: University Press, 1960.

Estep, William Roscoe. *The Anabaptist Story*. 3rd ed. Nashville: Broadman, 1996.

———. "Anabaptists, Baptists, and the Free Church Movement." *Criswell Theological Review* 6 (1993) 300–17.

———. "On the Origins of English Baptists." *Baptist History and Heritage* 22 (1987) 19–26.

———. "Thomas Helwys: Bold Architect of Baptist Policy on Church-State Relations." *Baptist History and Heritage* 20 (1985) 24–34.

Evans, Benjamin. *The Early English Baptists*. 2 vols. Greenwood, SC: Attic, 1977.

———. *The Early English Baptists*. Baptist History Collection 1. Version 1 [CD-ROM]. Paris, AR: Baptist Standard Bearer, 2005.

Fiddes, Paul. *Tracks and Traces: Baptist Identity in Church and Theology*. Studies in Baptist History and Thought. Eugene, OR: Wipf and Stock, 2007.

Firth, Katherine R. *The Apocalyptic Tradition in Reformation Britain, 1530–1645*. Oxford: Oxford University Press, 1979.

Foxe, John. *The Acts and Monuments*. 1563 ed. Online: https://www.johnfoxe.org/index. php?realm=text&edition=1563&gototype=.

———. *The Acts and Monuments*. 1570 ed. Online: http://www.johnfoxe.org/index.php? realm=text&gototype=modern&edition=1570&page id=2.

Friesen, Abraham. "Baptist Interpretations of Anabaptist History." In *Mennonites and Baptists*, 39–71. Winnipeg, Manitoba: Kindred, 1993.

Garrett, Christina. *The Marian Exiles: A Study in the Origins of Elizabethan Puritanism*. Cambridge, England: Cambridge University Press, 2010.

Garrett, James Leo, Jr. *Baptist Theology: A Four-Century Study*. Macon, GA: Mercer University Press, 2009.

———. "Restitution and Dissent Among Early English Baptists: Part II—Representative Late Sixteenth and Early Seventeenth Century Sources." *Baptist History and Heritage* 13 (1978) 11–27.

Gee, H., and W. J. Hardy. *Documents Illustrative of English Church History*. 1986. Repr., London: MacMillan, 1921.

George, Timothy. "Between Pacifism and Coercion: The English Baptist Doctrine of Religious Toleration." *Mennonite Quarterly Review* 58 (1984) 30–49.

———. "The English Baptists of the 17th Century." *Mennonite Quarterly Review* 58 (1984) 327–28.

Greaves, Richard L. "The Puritan-Nonconformist Tradition in England, 1560–1700: Historiographical Reflections." *Albion* 17.4 (1985) 449–86.

Griswold, Barbara Stone. "Congregational Dynamics in the Early Tradition of Independency." PhD diss., Baylor University, 2006.

Gulley, Thomas Kent. "The General Baptists in Early Stuart and Revolutionary England." PhD diss., University of Wisconsin-Madison, 1994.

Guy, J. A. "Henry VIII and the *Praemunire Manoeuvres* of 1530–1531." *English Historical Review* (1982) 481–503.

Harris, Lawrence Holiday. *The Origins and Growth of Baptist Faith: Twenty Baptist Trailblazers in World History*. Spartanburg, SC: Proprietary, 2001.

Haykin, Michael A. G. "Zeal to Promote the Common Good, The Story of the King James Bible." *Southern Baptist Journal of Theology* 15.4 (2011) 18–29.

Bibliography

Haymes, Brian. "On Religious Liberty: Re-Reading a *Short Declaration of the Mystery of Iniquity* in London in 2005." *Baptist Quarterly* 42 (2007) 197–217.

Helwys, Thomas. *An Advertisement or Admonition unto the Congregations, Which Men Call the New Frylers, in the Lowe Countries.* In *The Life and Writings of Thomas Helwys*, edited by Joe Early Jr., 93–154. Macon, GA: Mercer University Press, 2009.

———. *A Confession of the True English Church.* In *The Life and Writings of Thomas Helwys*, edited by Joe Early Jr., 60–64. Macon, GA: Mercer University Press, 2009.

———. *A Declaration of Faith of the English People Remaining at Amsterdam.* In *Baptist Confessions of Faith*, edited by William L. Lumpkin, 114–23. Valley Forge, PA: Judson, 1989.

———. *Objections Answered.* New York: Da Capo, 1973.

———. *A Short Declaration of the Mystery of Iniquity.* Classics of Religious Liberty 1. Macon, GA: Mercer University Press, 1998.

Hertzler, James R. "English Baptists Interpret Continental Mennonites in the Early Nineteenth Century." *Mennonite Quarterly Review* 54 (1980) 42–52.

Hill, Christopher. *Antichrist in the Seventeenth-Century England.* Oxford: Oxford University, 1971.

Hooker, Richard. *Of the Laws of Ecclesiastical Polity.* Vol. 8. Edited by Arthur Stephen McGrade. Cambridge: Cambridge University Press, 1989.

Horst, Irvin B. *The Radical Brethren: Anabaptism and the English Reformation to 1558.* Nieuwkoop: de Graff, 1972.

Hudson, Winthrop S. "Who Were the Baptists?" *Baptist Quarterly* 17 (1957) 303–12.

Jacob, Henry. *A Defense of the Churches and Ministry of Englande.* Middelburch: Engel, 1559.

Johnson, Stephen Monroe. "The Soteriology of the English General Baptists to 1630: A Study in Theological Kinship and Dependence." PhD diss., Westminster Theological Seminary, 1988.

Jordan, Wilbur Kitchener. *The Development of Religious Toleration in England from the Beginning of the English Reformation to the Death of Queen Elizabeth.* 4 vols. Cambridge, MA: Harvard University Press, 1932–1940.

Karlberg, Mark W. "Moses and Christ—The Place of Law in Seventeenth-Century Puritanism." *Trinity Journal* 10.1 (1989) 11–32.

Kirby, Torrance. "The Articles of Religion of the Church of England (1563/1571) Commonly Called the Thirty-Nine Articles." Online: http://people.mcgill.ca/files/torrance.kirby/39ArticlesRefBekennt2009.pdf.

———. "Lay Supremacy: Reform of the Canon Law of England from Henry VIII to Elizabeth I (1529–1571)." *Reformation and Renaissance Review: Journal of the Society for Reformation Studies* 8 (2006) 349–70.

Kliever, Lonnie D. "General Baptist Origins: The Question of Anabaptist Influence." *Mennonite Quarterly Review* 36 (1962) 291–321.

Kraus, C. Norman. "Anabaptist Influence on English Separatism as Seen in Robert Browne." *Mennonite Quarterly Review* 34 (1960) 5–19.

Lahey, Stephen E. *John Wyclif.* Oxford: Oxford University Press, 2009.

Lane, Daniel C. "Some Difficulties in Covenant Theology's View of Baptism as a Seal." *Bibliotheca Sacra* 165 (2008) 164–77.

Lee, Jason K. "Baptism and Covenant." In *Restoring Integrity in Baptist Churches*, edited by Thomas White, Jason G. Duesing, and Malcolm B. Yarnell III, 119–36. Grand Rapids: Kregel, 2008.

———. *The Theology of John Smyth: Puritan, Separatist, Baptist, Mennonite*. Macon, GA: Mercer University, 2003.

Loewen, Harry. "John Smyth's Congregation. English Separatism, Mennonite Influence, and the Elect Nation." *Journal of Mennonite Studies* 10 (1992) 218–20.

Luther, Martin. *Preface to the Revelation of St. John [I]*. Translated by Charles M. Jacobs. In *Luther's Works*, edited by Jaroslav Pelikan (vols. 1–30) and Helmut T. Lehmann (vols. 31–55), 35:339–411. Philadelphia: Muhlenberg, 1960.

———. *The Misuse of the Mass*. Translated by Frederick C. Ahrens. In *Luther's Works*, edited by Jaroslav Pelikan (vols. 1–30) and Helmut T. Lehmann (vols. 31–55), 36:127–230. Philadelphia: Muhlenberg, 1960.

———. "Temporal Authority (1523)." Online: http://pages.uoregon.edu/sshoemak/323/texts/luther~1.htm.

McBeth, Leon. "Baptist Beginnings." *Baptist History and Heritage* 15 (1980) 36–41.

———. *The Baptist Heritage: Four Centuries of Baptist Witness*. Nashville: Broadman, 1987.

McClendon, James W., Jr. "The Baptist and Mennonite Vision." In *Mennonites and Baptists: A Continuing Conversation*, edited by Paul Toews, 211–24. Winnipeg, Manitoba: Kindred, 1993.

McGiffert, Michael. "Grace and Works: The Rise and Division of Covenant Divinity in Elizabethan Puritanism." *Harvard Theological Review* 75.4 (1982) 463–502.

McKibbens, Thomas R. "Our Baptist Heritage in Worship." *Review & Expositor* 80 (1983) 53–69.

Monck, Thomas, and W. Madison Grace. "Transcriber's Preface to an Orthodox Creed: Unabridged 17th Century General Baptist Confession." *Southwestern Journal of Theology* 48 (2006) 127–82.

Morgan, Edmund S. *Visible Saints: The History of a Puritan Idea*. New York: Cornell University Press, 1965.

Newman, A. H. "The Reformation from a Baptist Point of View." *Baptist Quarterly* 6 (1884) 9.

Patterson, Paige. "Genetics versus Historiography: A Case for the Connections of the Continental Anabaptists and Contemporary Baptists." Paper presented at the annual meeting of the Evangelical Theological Society, New Orleans, LA, November 18, 2009.

Payne, Ernest Alexander. "Contacts between Mennonites and Baptists." *Foundations* 4 (1961) 39–55.

———. *Thomas Helwys and the First Baptist Church in England*. 2nd ed. London: Baptist Union of Great Britain & Ireland, 1966.

Phillips, J. Stephen. "Thomas Helwys and the Idea of Religious Liberty." PhD diss., Baylor University, 1998.

Pitts, William L. "Baptist Origins and Identity in 1609: The John Smyth/Richard Clifton Debate." *Perspectives in Religious Studies* 36 (2009) 377–90.

Pollard, A. F. *Wolsey*. London: Longmans, 1953.

Rankin, R. Andrew. "Baptist Origins: The Role of Aristotelianism in the Ecclesiology of John Smyth." *Fides et Historia* 28 (1996) 4–16.

Rex, Richard. *The Tudors*. Gloucestershire, UK: Tempus, 2005.

Rich, Antony D. "Thomas Helwys' First Confession of Faith: 1610." *Baptist Quarterly* 43 (2009) 235–41.

Bibliography

Ryrie, Alec. *The Age of Reformation: The Tudor and Stewart Realms 1485-1603*. London: Longman, 2009.

Saito, Goki. "An Investigation into the Relationship Between the Early English General Baptists and the Dutch Anabaptists." *Mennonite Quarterly Review* 54 (1980) 67–68.

The Schleitheim Confession. Translated and edited by John Yoder. Scottdale, PA: Herald, 1973.

Selement, George. "Covenant Theology of English Separatism and the Separation of Church and State." *Journal of the American Academy of Religion* 41 (1973) 66–74.

Sellers, Ian. "Edwardians, Anabaptists and the Problem of Baptist Origins." *Baptist Quarterly* 29 (1981) 97–112.

Shantz, Douglas H. "The Place of the Resurrected Christ in the Writings of John Smyth." *Baptist Quarterly* 30 (1984) 199–203.

Sharkey, Jessica. "Between King and Pope: Thomas Wolsey and the Knight Mission." *Historical Research* 84 (2011) 238.

Singleton, Robert, and W. J. Torrance Kirby. "Robert Singleton's Sermon at Paul's Cross in 1535: The 'True Church' and Royal Supremacy." *Reformation and Renaissance Review* 10 (2008) 343–68.

Smyth, John. *The Churches of the Separation*. English Experience 624. New York: Da Capo, 1973.

———. "Short Confession of Faith in XX Articles by John Smyth." In *Baptist Confessions of Faith*, edited by William L. Lumpkin, 97–101. Valley Forge, PA: Judson, 1989.

———. *The Works of John Smyth, Fellow of Christ's College, 1594–1598*. Edited by William T. Whitley. 2 vols. London: Cambridge University, 1915.

Solt, Leo F. *Church and State in Early Modern England*. Oxford: Oxford University, 1990.

Spalding, James C. "Restitution as a Normative Factor for Puritan Dissent." *Journal of the American Academy of Religion* 44 (1976) 47–63.

Sprunger, Keith and Mary. "The Church in the Bakehouse: John Smyth's English Anabaptist Congregation at Amsterdam, 1609–1660." *Mennonite Quarterly Review* 85 (2011) 219–58.

———. "The English Baptists of the 18th Century." *Mennonite Quarterly Review* 62 (1988) 181–82.

Stassen, Glen Harold. "Anabaptist Influence in the Origin of the Particular Baptists." *Mennonite Quarterly Review* 36 (1962) 322–48.

———. "Opening Menno Simons' Foundation-Book and Finding the Father of Baptist Origins Alongside the Mother-Calvinist Congregationalism." *Baptist History and Heritage* 33 (1998) 34–44.

———. "Revisioning Baptist Identity by Naming Our Origin and Character Rightly." *Baptist History and Heritage* 33 (1998) 45–54.

Stealey, Sydnor Lorenzo. *Baptist Treasury*. New York: Crowell, 1958.

Taylor, Adam. *The History of the English General Baptists*. The Baptist History Collection. Version 1 [CD-ROM]. Paris, AR: Baptist Standard Bearer, 2005.

Timmer, Kirsten Thea. "John Smyth's Request for Mennonite Recognition and Admission: Four Newly Translated Letters, 1610–1612." *Baptist History and Heritage* 44 (2009) 8–19.

Torbet, Robert G. *A History of the Baptists*. 3rd ed. Valley Forge, PA: Judson, 1973.

Towns, Lydia. "Faithfulness in the Face of Persecution: Thomas Helwys' Struggle for a Better World." *Baptist History and Heritage* 45 (2010) 80–91.

Trinterud, Leonard J. "The Origins of Puritanism." *Church History* 20.1 (1951) 37–57.

Underwood, A. C. *A History of English Baptists*. London: British Baptist Union, 1947.

Vedder, Henry C. *Short History of the Baptists*. Hong Kong: Baptist, 1954.

Von Rohr, John R. "Covenant and Assurance in Early English Puritanism." *Church History* 34 (1965) 195–203.

Wardin, Albert W. "Baptist Influences on Mennonite Brethren with an Emphasis on the Practice of Immersion." *Direction* 8 (1979) 33–38.

White, Barrington R. "Early Baptist Arguments for Religious Freedom: Their Overlooked Agenda." *Baptist History and Heritage* 24 (1989) 3–10.

———. *The English Baptists of the Seventeenth Century*. London: Baptist Historical Society, 1996.

———. *The English Puritan Tradition*. Nashville: Broadman, 1980.

———. "English Separatists and John Smyth Revisited." *Baptist Quarterly* 30 (1984) 344–47.

———. *The English Separatists Tradition: From the Marian Martyrs to the Pilgrim Fathers*. Oxford: Oxford University, 1971.

Whitley, William T. "Biography." In *The Works of John Smyth, Fellow of Christ's College, 1594–1598*, edited by William T. Whitley, 1:xvii–cxxii. London: Cambridge University Press, 1915.

———. *A History of the British Baptists*. London: Griffin, 1923.

Whittock, Martyn J. "Baptist Roots: The Use of Models in Tracing Baptist Origins." *Evangelical Quarterly* 57 (1985) 317–26.

———. "Continental Baptists and Early English Baptist." *Baptist Quarterly* 1 (1925) 24–36.

Wilkens, David. *Concilia Magnae Britanniae et Heberniae*. 4 vols. London: Gosling, Gyles, Woodward, and Davis, 1737.

Williams, George H. *The Radical Reformation*. Philadelphia: Westminster, 1962.

Wright, Stephen. *The Early English Baptists, 1603–1649*. Woodbridge, UK: Boydell, 2006.

———. "The Life and Writings of Thomas Helwys." *Baptist Quarterly* 43 (2010) 506–8.

Yarbrough, Slayden A. "The English Separatist Influence on the Baptist Tradition of Church-State Issues." *Baptist History and Heritage* 20 (1985) 14–23.

Yarnell, Malcolm B., III. *The Formation of Christian Doctrine*. Nashville: B. & H. Academic, 2007.

———. *Royal Priesthood in the English Reformation*. Oxford: Oxford University Press, 2014.

———. "'We Believe with the Heart and with the Mouth Confess': The Engaged Piety of the Early General Baptists." *Baptist Quarterly* 44 (2011) 1–23.

Subject Index

www.ingramcontent.com/pod-product-compliance
Lightning Source LLC
Chambersburg PA
CBHW050247041225
36306CB00031B/383